A PENNINE JOURNEY

A PENNINE JOURNEY

FROM SETTLE TO HADRIAN'S WALL IN WAINWRIGHT'S FOOTSTEPS

Edited by David Pitt

F

FRANCES LINCOLN LIMITED
PUBLISHERS

Frances Lincoln Ltd
4 Torriano Mews
Torriano Avenue
London NW5 2RZ
www.franceslincoln.com

CONTENTS

ACKNOWLEDGMENTS

There have been many people who have had a part in the production of this guide, so it is perhaps logical to pay tribute to them in chronological order.

Firstly to my father who, sixteen years after introducing me and my brothers to the Lake District on a family holiday in Grasmere in 1949, moved to Newby Bridge and through the medium of AW's Pictorial Guides familiarised himself with the fells. All his family were encouraged, on their visits, to join him on his walks. At the age of seventy-seven he thoroughly enjoyed accompanying me on my second long distance walk along the 81-mile Dales Way in 1979.

My wife Heather, who helped me to devise the route and who has been my constant companion on long distance walks since 1982, deserves the most praise and thanks. Without her support, particularly at an important juncture when I was hospitalised and she had to maintain contact with the original stage walkers and the test walkers to keep the project moving, this guide would not have materialised.

When we completed the walk in 1998 our friend, and fellow Wainwright Society member, Hilary Grayson encouraged us to write a guide to it. When our first attempt to find a sympathetic publisher failed, we abandoned the idea but resurrected it after the formation of the Wainwright Society. I broached the subject with Mark Richards, who led the Society's first organised walk from Grasmere over Fairfield in April 2003. Mark's books have guided me along the Offa's Dyke Path in 1980 and at various times between then and our walk along the Hadrian's Wall Path in 2006. Indeed part of this route is taken from the book he wrote jointly with Christopher Wright — *The Westmorland Heritage Walk*. His advice and help, when I was trying to meet the request of the Countryside Agency to safeguard, 'off season', the archaeology of that part of the route that touched on the Hadrian's Wall Path National

Trail, was much appreciated. It was as a result of his encouragement that I proposed the idea of a guide to the Wainwright Society committee and with the support and help of the secretary, Peter Linney, got their approval to launch the project.

Soon afterwards, I read in the next edition of the Wainwright Society's newsletter, *Footsteps*, about David Maughan, who independently had had the idea of writing a guide to the first part of the Pennine Journey, from Settle to Haltwhistle, using wherever possible Youth Hostels as overnight stops. I contacted him and he very kindly sent me all the extensive work he had done, which included his route descriptions and maps. Whilst this route differs in parts from David's route it inevitably shares many features and his advice, contribution, help and encouragement were very welcome.

Then I must express my thanks to all the rights of way officers, rangers and officials from the various County Councils, National Park Authorities and other agencies with whom this route has been discussed. Throughout weeks of discussions all were receptive to the idea of a new long distance footpath and were unstinting with their help and advice.

Now to the enthusiastic foot soldiers who have been the backbone of this campaign — by this I mean the volunteers who walked the stages. The route descriptions which they wrote or, in the case of test walkers, amended, sometimes incorporated sensible alternatives to the section of the route that they had been given. A roll call of everyone involved is included in the Appendix on page 224.

Finally a special mention must be made of the two people who have transformed the guide from, dare I say it, something pedestrian to something appealing and informative. Colin Bywater has done the excellent black/white sketches, of which half are his interpretation of those places on the Pennine Journey that coincide with places that AW sketched in some of his writings. Ron Scholes has done route maps that are AW-like in quality. In doing so he has walked every step of the way and could be considered to be the first Pennine Journeyman!

FOREWORD

One of the best reviews of *A Pennine Journey* said this: 'A marvellous account of a solitary journey by a man with a profound, even spiritual, love of the hills.'

No surprise there for Wainwright fans. We've all been captivated by that solitary presence and his profound understanding of remote places. What is odd about the review is that it appeared in *Good Housekeeping Magazine*. And there's a thought to make AW kick up the dust on Haystacks. Wainwright was to housekeeping what Herod was to nursery provision. In many ways he was an unworldly figure. Practicality was not his strong suit. It's a good job he never had a car because the garage bills would have bankrupted him. But what he lacked in the dubious black arts of DIY he more than made up for with his gentle insights and perceptive observation. And nowhere better that in A Pennine Journey. It's my favourite of all his books – the book that lay in a drawer for the neck end of fifty years until his editor at Michael Joseph, Jenny Dereham, persuaded him to publish it in 1986. (Except that's perhaps putting it a bit too strongly, given that nobody but Betty could ever persuade AW to do anything.) It was a book that charted a lonely, nervous journey from Settle to the Roman Wall and back again; a journey he made in autumn 1938 when Britain was on the brink of war.

'I wrote a book of my travels, not for others to see but to transport my thoughts to that blissful interlude of freedom.'

I only knew Wainwright as an old man when we were filming the television series for the BBC. But when I started to read A Pennine Journey I was suddenly introduced to a bolder, more visceral Wainwright.

Wainwright the Jack the lad with an eye for waitresses as well as wilderness. Wainwright experimenting, exploring ways of communicating his liberation by landscape. Wainwright challenging assumptions and suffering fools not at all.

Three people in his office at Blackburn Town Hall read the manuscript and said it was good but he still committed it to the drawer. He didn't have the confidence to publish it until his reputation had already been assured by the Pictorial Guides to the Lakeland Fells. No matter. The book is still as fresh today as when he wrote it. Even after the long gap, he changed nothing for publication. Not a word. The importance of A Pennine Journey is that it unlocks some of the secrets of his later, better known books. Read it, follow his trail and ever after you'll be able to catch glimpses of the young, vibrant Wainwright in the master fell walker of later years.

And now we can, more easily, follow in Wainwright's footsteps on his Pennine Journey thanks to the dedicated work of a team of Wainwright Society members led by David Pitt. For many months they devoted their spare time to exploring the modern footpaths and other rights of way that most closely follow the route Wainwright describes in his book. The result is this Pictorial Guide to A Pennine Journey.

Our hope is that this 247-mile walk in eighteen stages will become a popular long distance route, bringing the same economic benefits to communities along the way that *A Coast to Coast Walk* has already brought to many fragile rural economies across the north of England.

Eric Robson
Chairman, The Wainwright Society

INTRODUCTION

The genesis of this long distance footpath and accompanying walking guide is the book that Alfred Wainwright (henceforth to be known as AW) wrote in 1939, which, when it was published eventually in 1986, was entitled *A Pennine Journey: The Story of a Long Walk in 1938*. In his foreword to the book AW says that he wrote it in the months following his completion of the walk in October 1938, showed it to some colleagues in his office in the Treasurer's Department at Blackburn Town Hall and then put it away. However, Hunter Davies in his excellent biography says that AW seems to have had ambitions to have the book published under the title *Pennine Campaign* but these were probably stifled by the onset of the Second World War. By the time it was published, I had become a firm AW admirer, having walked the Coast to Coast Walk in 1978 – a walk that started a sequence of annual long distance footpath walks that has continued to the present day with, hopefully, more annual walks to come. I had, with my wife Heather, already completed our first 'Wainwright Round' and whilst I found the book fascinating I did not think it relevant to what had become our main interest – that of long distance footpath walking. In the winter of 1991–2 Heather and I were debating what was to be our next long distance footpath, when I remembered the following extract from the introduction to AW's Coast to Coast Walk pictorial guide in which he encourages long distance footpath walkers to 'devise with the aid of maps their own cross-country marathons and not be merely followers of other people's routes'.

What we started to plan that winter, but did not complete until 1998 following a move to the Lake District in 1993, was our 'own cross-country marathon'. Whilst, technically, it does not follow 'other people's routes', nevertheless it is unashamedly based on AW's 'Pennine Journey'. We devised a route, using our maps and guide books of the area, which would take us to as many of the places AW mentioned in his book as reasonably possible, using public rights of way and not the roads that he used in 1938 – a route that AW might have chosen if he was planning it today. Then country roads could be used by walkers without too much danger – sixty years (and now seventy years) later it was quite a different kettle of fish!

At the first Annual General Meeting in 2004 of the recently formed Wainwright Society I asked whether the committee would consider utilising the route that Heather and I had devised as the basis of a collaborative Society members' initiative to complete a guide book based on *A Pennine Journey*. In early 2005 the idea was accepted and the project was launched at that year's Annual General Meeting. In 1998 we had used a motor caravan and car and were thus self sufficient as regards food and accommodation but the same could not be said for anyone following in our footsteps. A revision of our route was clearly needed so that some accommodation and sustenance was available at the end of each day's walk. The amended route is 247 miles long and divided into eighteen stages.

Volunteers to walk the eighteen stages, and to write appropriate route descriptions, were readily forthcoming. All were encouraged to suggest possible route revisions based, hopefully, on their own experience of the area. As a result, the amount of road walking was reduced markedly and in places a better route resulted. The revised routes were then distributed to a larger group of test walkers (which included many of the original volunteers) who then walked each stage again to see if the route descriptions could be followed without too many false steps. Finally the route maps and descriptions were sent out to the National Park authorities, County Councils, the Countryside Agency (now Natural England) and any other bodies that might want to comment on the impact of a new long distance footpath in their area. Once their observations had been received and taken on board the route descriptions were re-written into one common format.

When AW walked his Pennine Journey, long distance footpaths as we know them today did not exist. AW wrote the definitive guide for the first National Trail, the Pennine Way, in 1968, and since then there has been a steady growth in the number of paths (LDPs for short) that have been created. The Long Distance Walkers Association's latest handbook (2002) lists over 600 walks of over 20 miles that have sprung up as a result of initiatives by government, local government, national bodies such as the Ramblers Association and other like-minded organisations. The latest significant addition is the Pennine Bridleway, a 350-mile National Trail for horse riders and walkers from Derbyshire to Northumberland which should be completed in 2010. This Pennine Journey meets this within a mile of its start and does so again towards the end of the Journey.

From the charming market town of Settle the route takes you successively into the valleys of the rivers Wharfe, Ure and Swale before crossing the bleak moorland around Tan Hill to arrive at the historic town of Bowes. The name of the late Queen Mother, Elizabeth Bowes-Lyon, has its origin here. After Bowes the valleys of the Tees, Wear and Tyne, with their more industrial legacies, are met before arriving at the ancient town of Hexham with its magnificent Abbey. Soon you will be at Hadrian's Wall which was, for AW, the high spot of his journey. Here you will pick up the Hadrian's Wall Path National Trail for the next 24 miles to Greenhead. This is really one of the parts of the journey to savour. Rich in history with two major Roman forts at Chesters (Cilurnum) and Housesteads (Vircovicium) to explore as well as the sites of milecastles and turrets. It does not take much imagination to get the sense of being on the extreme edge of the Roman Empire.

At Greenhead the route heads south for Alston, one of the highest towns in England, before crossing the Pennines below its highest point of Cross Fell to enter the Eden Valley. The River Eden is Cumbria's longest river and for many people, its most beautiful. You will pass through pretty villages and the towns of Appleby and Kirkby Stephen before leaving the valley shortly after passing between Mallerstang Edge on one side of the narrowing vale and the dramatically named Wild Boar Fell. En route there are opportunities to see some of the Eden Benchmarks – ten sculptures commissioned for the Millennium and situated close to the river.

Then we enter an area that AW described in great detail in his pictorial guides *Walks in Limestone Country* and *Walks on the Howgill Fells*. From the head waters of the Eden we make our way to the valley of the River Rawthey, follow the river to Sedbergh and then cross to Dentdale. After Dent we are back in Three Peaks territory and our path takes us over two of them – Whernside and Ingleborough – before journey's end back in Settle.

Before setting out on this walk do buy and read AW's book. Whilst, necessarily, this guide does not follow his route it is only after absorbing yourself in his narrative that you will be able to appreciate the circumstances and conditions under which the book was written and in doing so maximise the benefits of your journey.

Finally, how should the walk be planned? It can be done in a variety of ways. As a single walk it would take two and a half weeks. Alternatively, it could be divided into two, as its halfway point is just past Housesteads on Hadrian's Wall – AW's primary objective. Thirdly it splits neatly into three equal stages – to Westgate through dales and moorland; a section with Hadrian's Wall as its centrepiece before crossing the Pennines to Milburn; then the final stage being a return down the Eden Valley and eventually to Settle.

'. . . this [is] a walk that should be done in comfort and for pleasure or not at all.'

SCOTLAND

Kielder Water

NORTH SEA

R. N.TYNE

R. S. TYNE

Greenhead

Hexham

Newcastle-upon-Tyne

Sunderland

R. DERWENT

Carlisle

Alston

R. EDEN

R. WEAR

Penrith

Middleton-in-Teesdale

LAKE DISTRICT

Appleby

R. TEES

Middlesbrough

IRISH SEA

Bowes

R. SWALE

Kendal

Sedbergh

Askrigg

Northallerton

R. LUNE

Buckden

R. URE

Settle

R. NIDD

York

Lancaster

R. WHARFE

R. AIRE

Leeds

R. RIBBLE

Preston

NORTHERN ENGLAND

A PENNINE JOURNEY -----
IN RELATION TO THE REGION'S MAJOR RIVERS

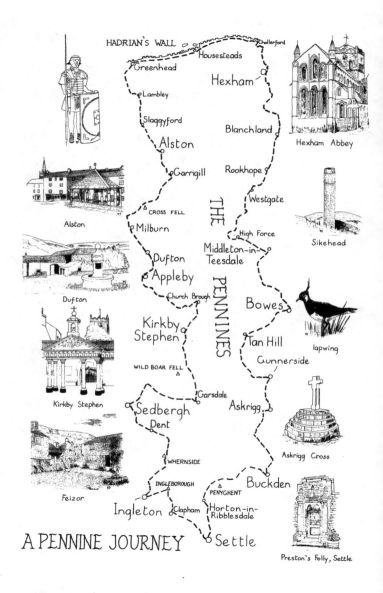

HADRIAN'S WALL · Chollerford

Greenhead
Housesteads

Hexham

Lambley

Slaggyford

Alston

Blanchland

Garrigill

Rookhope

Westgate

△ CROSS FELL

Milburn

High Force

Dufton

Middleton-in-Teesdale

Appleby

Church Brough

Bowes

Kirkby Stephen

Tan Hill

WILD BOAR FELL △

Gunnerside

Garsdale

Askrigg

Sedbergh

Dent

△ WHERNSIDE

INGLEBOROUGH △

△ PENYGHENT

Buckden

Ingleton

Clapham

Horton-in-Ribblesdale

THE PENNINES

Settle

Alston

Dufton

Kirkby Stephen

Feizor

Hexham Abbey

Sikehead

lapwing

Askrigg Cross

Preston's Folly, Settle

A PENNINE JOURNEY

KEY - SIGN REFERENCES

(signs and abbreviations used in the maps)

Road

Track

Walking Routes

MAIN ROUTE : - - - - - - -

OTHER ROUTES : - - - - -

Bridge

Church +

Building

Woods

    conifer

    deciduous

Crag

Boulders

Limestone pavement

Roman Wall

  masonry

  vallum

  ditch

Map scale : 2½" = 1 mile

North is top of the page

Railway

River , Stream

Wall

Broken wall

Fence

Hedge

Footbridge   FB

Way marker   WM

Youth Hostels Association

    YHA △

Contours (at 100' intervals)

    800
    900

Summit   ●

Ordnance Survey Column

  with O.S number

  (triangulation point)

Miles (from starting point)
and direction of route

    (48)

PW - Pennine Way

RS

DAY ONE

Settle to Horton in Ribblesdale

Distance	7¼ miles
Highest Point	1,302 feet
Height Ascended	1,824 feet
Going	Moderate
Map	O.S. Explorer OL2

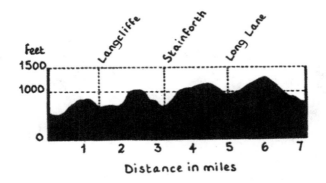

The Pennine Journey starts at one of the places which, in recent years, has helped to consolidate Settle's reputation – the station at the start of the well-known Settle to Carlisle railway. If time permits then the train journey to/from Carlisle either at the start of the Pennine Journey or at the end offers a delightful, scenic trip through the beautiful countryside of the Ribble Valley and over the magnificent Ribblehead Viaduct. The journey continues through the Eden Valley to the historic city of Carlisle – the major Roman settlement on Hadrian's Wall. The Wall was the primary objective of AW when he set out from Settle on his Pennine Journey.

The relatively short stage today provides an excellent opportunity to explore the charms of Settle, one of the most delightful market towns of the Yorkshire Dales. Settle, although just outside the boundary of the Yorkshire Dales National Park, is an ideal centre for walkers of all ages and capabilities — 'a gateway to the hills'. It is a busy and quaint town of narrow streets and shady corners in a confusion of old stone cottages and houses and serves the rural area of upper Ribblesdale.

Settle Station

It is seen at its best on a sunny market day (Tuesday) when the market square which fronts the busy A65 road is crammed with stalls and the two-storey Shambles provides an attractive focal point. There is an interesting Town Trail, two museums for those with time (and energy) to spare and, before leaving, take a look at the café facing the market square with a 1633 sign called, intriguingly, Naked Man.

During the day our path will join two long distance footpaths. The first is the Pennine Bridleway, a new 350-mile National Trail for walkers, cyclists and horse riders from Derbyshire to Northumberland, which should be substantially completed by 2010. The second is the Ribble Way, from the river's source on Gayle Moor close to the Ribblehead Viaduct to the salt marshes of Longton near Preston. The route soon arrives at the pretty village of Langcliffe, 'a quiet village set around a pleasant green', once famous for the tanning of leather. Opposite the telephone box, a sign on a house attests to its origins as an inn called Naked Woman – presumably a friend of Settle's Naked Man!

Stepping Stones, Stainforth

Before long the very quiet village of Stainforth is reached. This pre-Conquest settlement is a compact, attractive community divided by Stainforth Beck with stepping stones across it for Pennine Journey walkers.

The stage ends in Horton in Ribblesdale – a much bigger community – which is a Mecca for Three Peaks walkers, Pennine Wayfarers and pot-holers. The approach to Horton from the south is dominated by St Oswald's church, which dates from the reign of King Stephen.

Route Description

The start of this Pennine Journey is the bridge linking the platforms at Settle station over which AW walked after alighting from the train from Blackburn on 24 September 1938. Leave the station and at the bottom of the approach road turn right to the town centre. Upon reaching the main street (Duke Street) turn left, then right up Cheapside and go around Lloyds TSB bank. Head up a short stretch of cobbled road (Castle Hill), turning left when the metalled road is reached and then right up Constitution Hill. Leave this very soon on a rough, stony walled track (FP Langcliffe 1½m) – this is Banks Lane and is part of the Settle Loop of the Pennine Bridleway. Climb up the track until a gate is reached, ignore a path on the right (FP Malham) and continue straight ahead, with Penyghent on the skyline, keeping to the right hand side of the wall. Langcliffe soon comes into view down below to the left. Take a wall stile and go through a gate in the facing wall corner. Proceed through two more gates on a well-defined path and turn left on reaching the road into Langcliffe. The school is immediately visible on the right and between it and the Langcliffe Institute (with its very pointed spire) is a path (FP Stainforth 1½m). Take it and shortly pass some houses and Hope Hill Farm. Soon, when the walled track ceases, follow the footpath sign through the gate on the right hand side. The path climbs the facing limestone crag and continues beyond it and over two wall stiles until a lane is met. Turn left, pass through the farm buildings at Lower Winskill and go over three more wall stiles. From here there is a panoramic view that takes in both Ingleborough and Penyghent and if walking in late May/early June there are wild orchids and primroses to be seen.

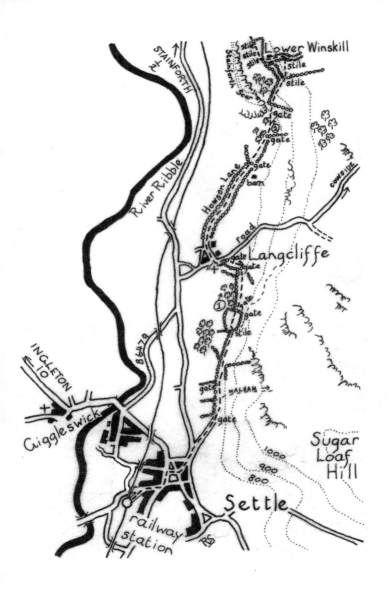

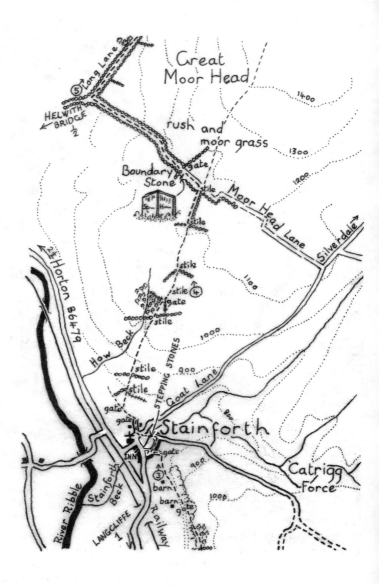

The path now descends the scar steeply through a wood, with a drop of about 150 feet down limestone steps which require great care particularly when wet. At a kissing gate turn right following a fence on the right. Yellow way-posts show the way into Stainforth where the Craven Heifer awaits thirsty and hungry walkers. On reaching the road turn right at Croft House (FP Goat Scar Lane) and continue for a short way through the village until the Green is reached. Take the left fork and cross the beck using the stepping stones. Cross over the road, take the track opposite and at the facing white gates turn right up the lane and over a wall stile into a meadow. At the first gate take the footpath that

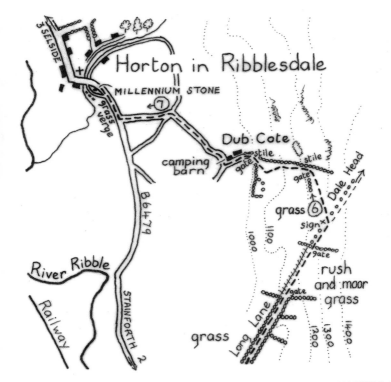

goes half right uphill to a wall stile on the horizon. Follow the clear path over five more wall stiles to reach the track of Moor Head Lane and turn left. A path opposite (FP Long Lane 1¾m) across the moor seems to offer a short cut but ignore it. Pass a boundary stone and at a fork turn right along Long Lane (FP Dale Head 2m).

After a steady uphill climb, turn left down a delightful green track to Dub Cote. At the camping barn turn right down the road, left upon joining another road and soon right again at the fork. Continue down to the B6479 Settle to Horton in Ribblesdale road, and turn right on meeting this towards Horton, using the roadside verge as there is no footpath. On the village green there is a Millennium Stone, placed there by Horton Flower Club — a fitting end to the first stage of this Pennine Journey.

DAY TWO

Horton in Ribblesdale to Buckden

Distance	12¾ miles
Highest Point	1,952 feet
Height Ascended	2,218 feet
Going	Moderate with one steep climb
Map	O.S. Explorer OL2 & OL30

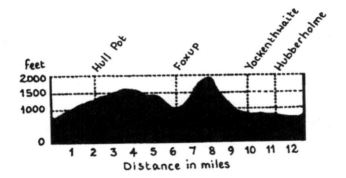

For long distance footpath walkers, Horton in Ribblesdale marks the junction of the Pennine Way, the Ribble Way and, now, the Pennine Journey, but for endurance walkers it is the traditional start and finish of one of the most famous ones – the 24-mile Three Peaks Walk over the summits of Whernside, Ingleborough and Penyghent. Later, on Days 17 and 18, the route will take us over Whernside and Ingleborough on paths described by AW in his book *Walks in Limestone Country*.

Horton in Ribblesdale is one of the leading centres in Great Britain for caving and pot-holing. North of the village are Alum Pot and the Long Churn cave system and on the western side of Penyghent are Hunt Pot and Hull Pot. Today's route passes Hull Pot

St Oswald's Church, Horton in Ribblesdale

which, at 300 feet in length and 60 feet in width and depth, is the largest hole in the country.

Initially, the route joins the Pennine Way along an ancient drove road (Horton Scar Lane) on to Foxup Moor, passing Hull Pot, before dropping down to Foxup Bridge in the quiet valley of Littondale. It then goes through the small hamlet of Halton Gill, which, like many others in the Yorkshire Dales, had its own chapel and enough children for its own school. Here an old track over the Horse Head Pass, from where AW saw a 'superb' panorama at sunset, leads to Yockenthwaite in Wharfedale.

For the remainder of this stage to Buckden the route follows the Dales Way. Before arriving in Buckden the path passes through the pretty hamlet of Hubberholme with the church of St Michael's and All Angels on one side of the river and the hostelry of the George Inn on the other. AW said that 'Hubberholme was delightful' and his view was shared by the author J.B. Priestley, who described Hubberholme as 'one of the smallest and pleasantest places in the

Hull Pot

world'. Not surprisingly his ashes are buried here. Scar House just above Hubberholme was visited twice by the Quaker George Fox on his travels during the second half of the seventeenth century.

Route Description

From the millennium stone on the village green go past the church and through the village for a short while until a sign (BW Foxup 5½m) points to a track on the right — it is at this point that the Pennine Way arrives at Horton. Follow this track between stone walls until it emerges on the fellside at a junction of paths, with the right hand one being the Pennine Way's descent from Penyghent passing close to Hunt Pot. Continue straight ahead to arrive soon at the very impressive Hull Pot with its feeder stream of Hull Pot Beck (only visible during wet periods). After stopping to admire this huge chasm from a safe distance, bear right and take the stile over the wall to pass the more modest High Hull Pot, where a stream disappears into the ground. At a wall corner continue ahead with the wall on the right.

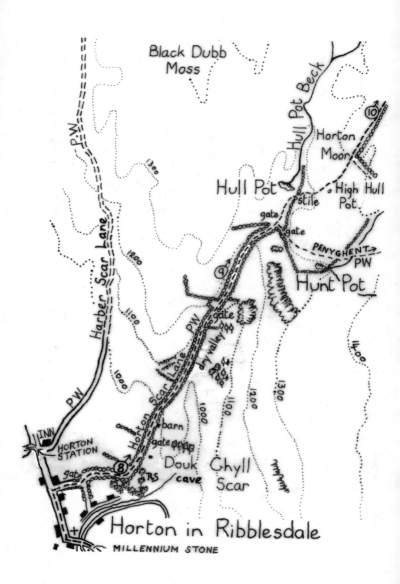

Black Dubb
Moss

Hull Pot Beck

PW

10

Horton
Moor

1300

Hull Pot

stile

High Hull
Pot

gate

gate

PENYGHENT
PW

PW

1200

Harber Scar Lane

9

Hunt Pot

1100

gate

PW

1000

Horton Scar Lane

dry valley

1300

1200

INN

HORTON
STATION

barn

gate gate

1000

1100

PW

gate

8

RS

Douk
cave

Ghyll
Scar

1100

Horton in Ribblesdale

MILLENNIUM STONE

Pass through a gate, go forward through a cross wall and over a small bridge. The path, damp in places, broadly contours around Penyghent and Plover Hill to meet another cross wall. Go through the gate and, after passing a path off right (FP Plover Hill), go through a further gate (FP Horton in Ribblesdale 3¾m; Foxup 1¾m).

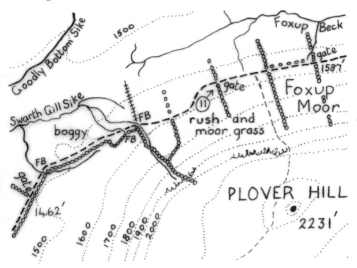

This is now what the O.S. map describes as Foxup Road, which soon starts to descend gradually, passing through a succession of gates with Foxup then Halton Gill coming into view. Drop down to Foxup and meet the metalled road at Foxup Bridge Farm. Turn right and follow the road towards Halton Gill.

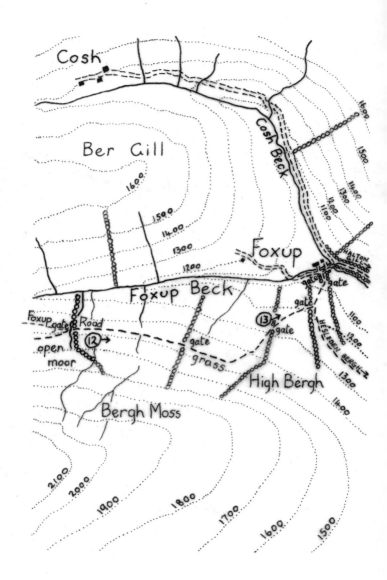

Cosh

Ber Gill

Cosh Beck

160.0.

150.0.

140.0.

1600.

1500.

1400.

1300.

1200.

1100.

Foxup

HALTON GILL

1300.
1200.
1100.

gate

gate

gate

Foxup Beck

1200.

1300.

gate

(13)

gate

gate

HESLDEN BERGH

1100.

1200.

1300.

1400.

Foxup gate Road

(12)

open
moor

gate

gate

grass

High Bergh

Bergh Moss

2100.

2000.

1900.

1800.

1700.

1600.

1500.

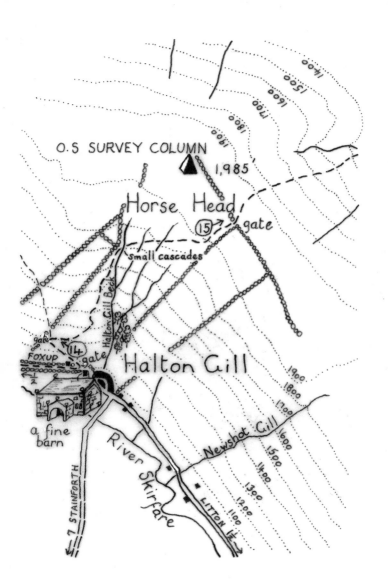

O.S SURVEY COLUMN

1,985

Horse Head

15 gate

small cascades

Halton Gill Beck

gate

Foxup

14

gate

Halton Gill

a fine barn

River Skirfare

Newshot Gill

1900
1800
1700
1600
1500
1400
1300
1200
1100

LITTON I↑

7 STAINFORTH

7
½

1400
1500
1600
1700
1800
1900

After a converted barn, look out on the left for a sign (FP Beckermonds 2½m, Yockenthwaite 3m) on to an old track over the Horse Head Pass and at the first junction take the right hand fork. The path continues its near 1,000-foot climb to Horse Head Gate, passing a small, attractive waterfall on the right. At the ridge wall pass through the gate with the trig point of Horse Head (1,985ft) on the left but before descending look back to Plover Hill and the more distant Penyghent. The path drops steadily before crossing a small tributary of Hagg Beck.

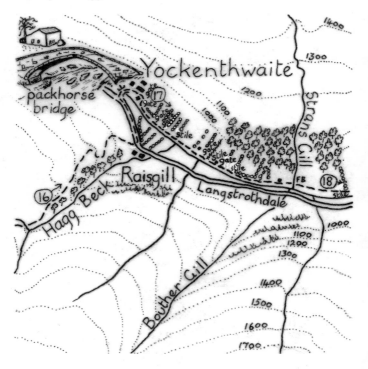

The track now parallels Hagg Beck for the remainder of the descent down to the road at Raisgill in Langstrothdale. This is the major one of two valleys that branch off the head of Wharfedale.

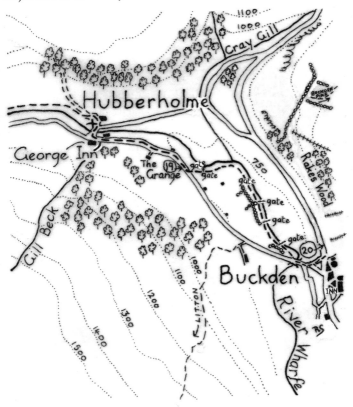

The river that has been in view for a large part of the descent is the infant River Wharfe. Turn left along the road to the bridge over the river at Yockenthwaite with its post box, cross the bridge and turn right to pass in front of the farmhouse. Go over a stile with a steep drop to descend to and follow the delightful riverside path. This is now the Dales Way, an 81-mile footpath from Ilkley to Bowness on Windermere, to be followed as far as Buckden.

The well-signed path leads to the lovely church at Hubberholme and then crosses the bridge to the George Inn. It hardly seems possible that this bridge was once on a busy coaching route from Lancaster to Newcastle. Take the road left until a footpath sign points back to the river bank for the remaining stretch into Buckden where the Buck Inn awaits.

DAY THREE

Buckden to Gunnerside

Distance	17½ miles
Highest Point	1,841 feet
Height Ascended	2,966 feet
Going	Moderate with one steep climb
Map	O.S. Explorer OL30

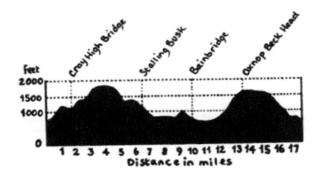

Buckden is a peaceful and attractive village that is delightfully situated in a large arena where the flat, glaciated valley of the River Wharfe narrows into Langstrothdale. In the eighteenth century Buckden became a prosperous lead mining community but its name denotes much earlier origins. Buckden, whose name is said to be derived from being a 'valley frequented by bucks', was part of the vast hunting forest of Langstrothdale and is dominated by Buckden Pike (2,302ft). For those with energy to spare then the ascent of Buckden Pike at the start of the day's stage would give wonderful views of a large part of the day's walk.

After contouring around Buckden Pike, the route crosses the plateau of high ground between Bishopdale and Raydale on an old drove road and then passes through Stalling Busk to Semer Water.

Waterfalls above Cray

Formed by the last glacier that carved out Wensleydale, AW likened
it to 'a flooded field' – a view possibly coloured by his memories
of Windermere. The picturesque village of Bainbridge with its huge
village green is soon reached.

Bainbridge Green

Half an hour or so later is Askrigg, which featured prominently in the TV series *All Creatures Great and Small*. In the centre of the village, near Askrigg church, is the building that became 'Skeldale House' the surgery/home of James Herriott. The stiff climb out of Wensleydale, which 'taxed my tired limbs sorely', levels out at Askrigg Common. Soon Swaledale comes into view and the descent into this most lovely valley is by a track along Oxnop Scar to the former lead mining community of Gunnerside.

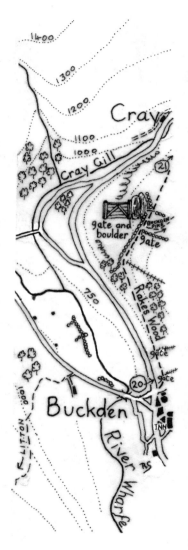

Route Description

Leave the car park at the northern edge of the village through a gate at the far end and take the well-graded Buckden Rake – a Roman road. The route has now joined the Lady Anne Clifford's Way – a 100-mile footpath from Skipton to Penrith. The track climbs gradually above Buckden Wood, traverses the north west flanks of Buckden Out Moor and reaches the road near Cray High Bridge.

Look to the right on approaching the road and admire the series of small waterfalls cascading down the fellside. Turn right along the road and leave it on the left on the unmistakeable track of Gilbert Lane (FP Stalling Busk 4½m). AW described this track as 'a walkers' way par excellence'. Looking back Buckden Pike increases in stature while ahead the track zigzags up the fellside. Initially it is a stiff climb but on a good wide track – look out for a glimpse of Penyghent to the south-west from near Cray Moss.

After passing the limestone pavement at Stake Moss, the route crosses the plateau along a

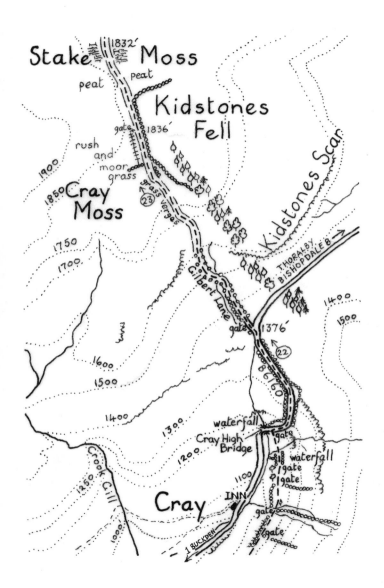

Stake Moss

1832'

peat   peat

Kidstones
Fell

gate   1836'

rush
and
moor
grass

Cray
Moss

grass verges

23

1900

1850

1750

1700

Kidstones Scar

THORALBY
BISHOPDALE 8

Gilbert Lane

gate   1376'

22

B 6160

1400

1500

1600

1500

1400

1300

1200

waterfall

Cray High
Bridge

gate

waterfall
gate
gate

Crook Gill

1250

1100

Cray   INN

gate

gate

1 BUCKDEN

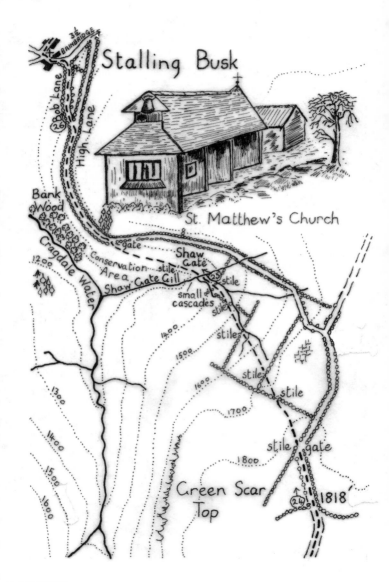

Stalling Busk

St. Matthew's Church

½ BAINBRIDGE

Bob Lane

High Lane

Bank Wood

Cragdale Water

1200

Conservation Area

gate

Shaw Gate

stile

Shaw Gate Gill

25

stile

stile

small cascades

stile

stile

1400

stile

1500

stile

1300

1600

stile

1400

1700

1500

stile

stile gate

1600

1800

Green Scar Top

24

1818

walled drove road which is left at a ladder stile when the main track (and the Lady Anne Clifford's Way) turns away to the north-east. The path drops down to Shaw Gate and passes close to a sequence of archaeological sites well worth closer investigation if so inclined – an interpretive display gives more information about this Site of Special Scientific Interest (SSSI). Soon the path meets High Lane, which is followed until the stony track of Bob Lane descends into Stalling Busk. Turn left at the metalled Butts Lane to enter this lovely, small village.

Its principal feature is St Matthew's Church which has an unusual design. Once past the church follow a sign pointing downhill to the

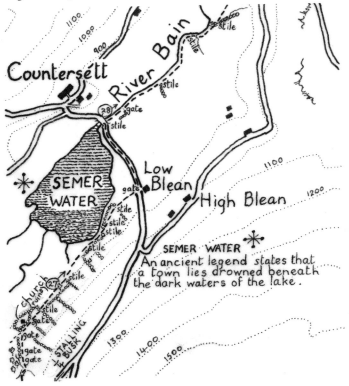

SEMER WATER
An ancient legend states that a town lies drowned beneath the dark waters of the lake.

earlier ruined church built originally in the early 1600s. The path leads down to Semer Water and follows the eastern shore to meet the road at Low Blean. Turn left and, just before the bridge over the River Bain, take the path on the right by the river but leave it at a ladder stile. The River Bain, at 2½ miles in length, is reputedly England's shortest river. Go up a gentle slope across a meadow, pass a stone barn with a view of the river in its steeply wooded glen and ascend Bracken Hill ahead. As the path descends there is a good panorama of Wensleydale with the earthworks of the Roman fort of Virosidum clearly visible. Ignore a stile/gate leading to the minor road and continue downhill, with a good view of the river, to meet the main road. Turn left into Bainbridge – a fine, picturesque village with spacious green and medieval stocks which

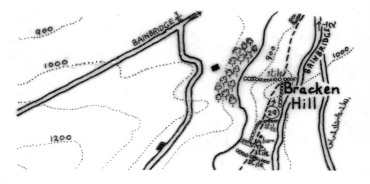

were used in the reign of Queen Elizabeth I. Leave the village on the Askrigg road passing the Rose and Crown. Once over the River Ure take a path on the right (FP Askrigg 1m) which leads on to a disused railway track. Take a path on the left to join the adjacent road opposite the village primary school and head towards the village but soon follow a paved footpath on the left leading across two fields. Go through a wicket gate in the corner to pass a row of cottages and enter the churchyard. Go through the village and at a fork in the road, where the route again meets the Lady Anne Clifford's Way, take the lane to Muker.

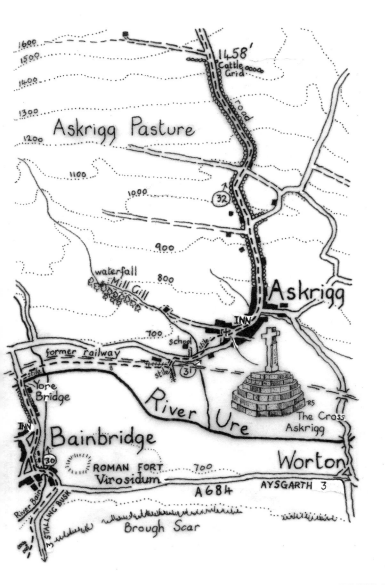

1600
1500
1400

1300

Askrigg Pasture

1200

1100

1000

900

800

waterfall
Mill Gill

700

former railway

Yore Bridge

stile

stile

school

stile

1458'
Cattle Grid

road

A32

Askrigg

INN

31

River Ure

INN

Bainbridge

B30

ROMAN FORT
Virosidum

River Bain

STALLING BUSK

Brough Scar

The Cross
Askrigg

RS

Worton

700

A684

AYSGARTH 3

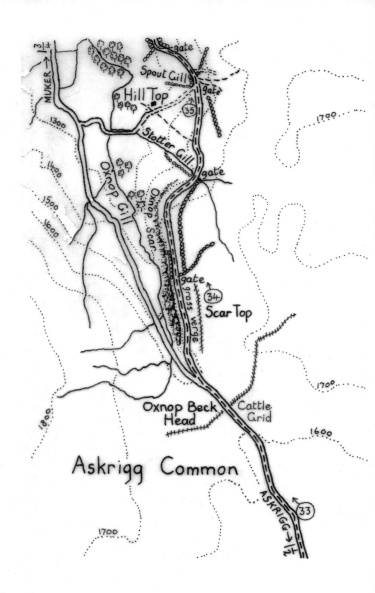

A long stretch of road walking follows, climbing around 900 feet and steep in places, to a cattle grid. Here, look back for good views of Wensleydale and in particular Semer Water and the valley of the River Bain. Cross Askrigg Common before starting the descent into Swaledale. Shortly after the cattle grid at Oxnop Beck Head leave the road for a metalled track on the right which skirts the edge of Oxnop Scar. This winds its way down past Stotter Gill, Spout Gill and Gill Head becoming a fully metalled lane before it meets the main road at Satron. Turn right along the road and then cross the beautiful River Swale with the village of Gunnerside (and the Kings Head) only a few hundred yards away.

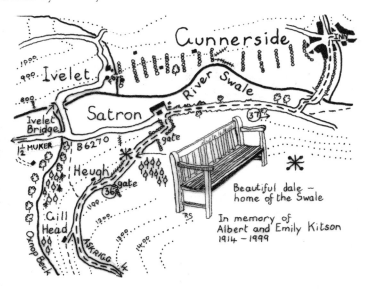

Beautiful dale – home of the Swale

In memory of Albert and Emily Kitson 1914 – 1999

DAY FOUR

Gunnerside to Bowes

Distance	17½ miles
Highest Point	1,778 feet
Height Ascended	2,146 feet
Going	Moderate
Map	O.S. Explorer OL30 & OL31

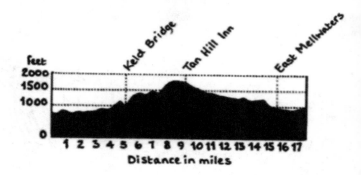

Gunnerside, on the site of an Old Norse settlement, is a small village at the heart of Swaledale. In AW's *Pennine Way Companion*, written in 1968, he describes Swaledale as 'the most beautiful of the Yorkshire Dales' with Wharfedale as his second choice. This, however, is a reversal of the opinion expressed in his earlier *A Pennine Journey*. In the hills to the north of the river, chiefly in the triangle of land formed by Swaledale and Arkengarthdale, lead had been mined since the Romans but the industry had its heyday in the seventeenth to the nineteenth centuries. AW comments that 'another Klondyke arose in these wild hills' and was clearly fascinated enough to take his Coast to Coast Walk through the area on the section from Keld to Reeth.

East Gill Force

The path initially follows the river through delightful meadows, past the outskirts of Muker, before climbing out of the valley to meet, just after the splendid falls of Kisdon Force 'where the Swale leaps along a very wooded ravine between sheer walls of gleaming limestone', the Pennine Way. For the remainder of the day the Pennine Way is followed but on the outskirts of Keld is joined by the Coast to Coast Walk for a very short stretch before striking out across bleak moorland to reach the Tan Hill Inn, at 1,732 feet the highest public house in Great Britain.

Tan Hill Inn

More desolate countryside follows as the path makes its way across Sleightholme Moor before there is a temporary parting of the ways. The Pennine Way heads north but the Pennine Journey uses the 'Bowes Loop' to reach the end of this stage at Bowes Castle.

Route Description

From the crossroads in the village take the lane that goes past the small green, with flower beds and two seats, and terminates at a pair of bungalows (Flatlands). A gate to the right of the large gate has a footpath sign: take the paved path around and to the back of the right hand bungalow where a gap stile leads to a meadow path. Follow this through mainly gap stiles to the small community of Ivelet. Turn left down the road to Ivelet Bridge over the Swale and take a riverside path on the right before the bridge is crossed. This delightful path is by, or close to, the river and soon after the stile beyond Ramps Holme Farm look out for a fork in the path, taking the left hand branch which descends to Ramps Holme Bridge.

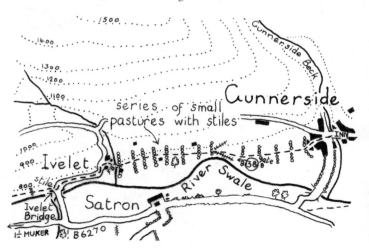

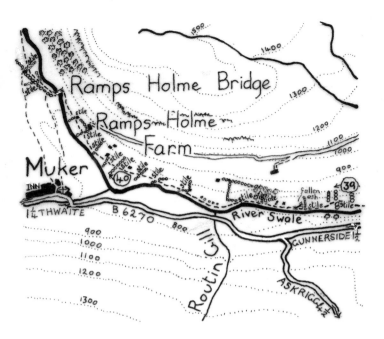

Once over the bridge ignore the paved path which heads back towards Muker and take the path heading north. This stays close to the river and as it climbs up to meet the Pennine Way, look out for a gap in the wall on the right where a path leads to a viewpoint for Kisdon Force – a splendid waterfall and worthwhile diversion. Within a few minutes of meeting the Pennine Way, Keld Bridge is reached – a significant junction for all AW enthusiasts being the meeting of the Pennine Way and the Coast to Coast Walk, and now the Pennine Journey. Cross the bridge and continue along the Pennine Way by the attractive falls of East Gill Force – a celebratory photograph here would be highly appropriate. Turn left and follow the Pennine Way as it climbs up the slopes of Black Moor.

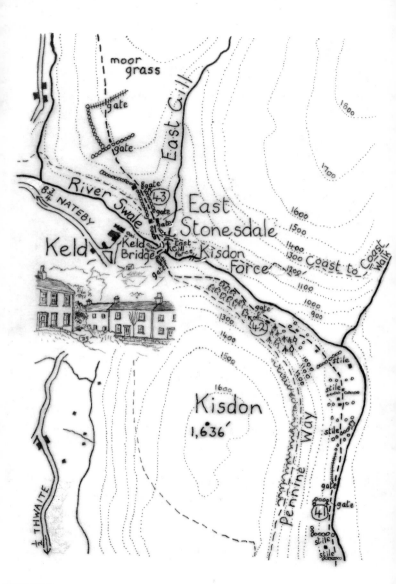

moor
grass

East Gill

gate

gate

1800

1700

River Swale

83
84 NATEBY

gate
43

gate
gate

East
Stonesdale

1600

1500

1400 Coast to Coast Walk
1300
1200

Keld

Keld
Bridge

East
Gill
Force

gate

Kisdon
Force

1100

1000
900

1300
42

1400

Kisdon
1,636′

1600

1500

stile

stile

stile

Pennine Way

gate
41 gate

stile

stile

½ THWAITE

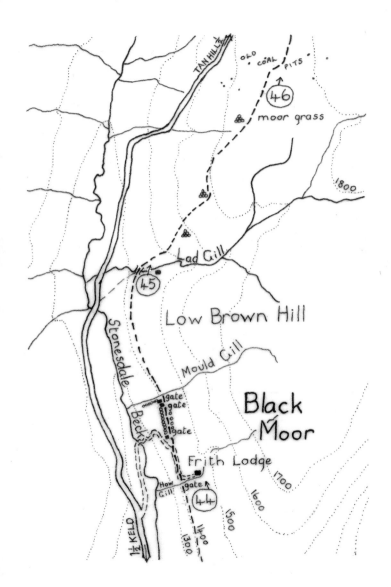

TAN HILL

OLD COAL PITS

↑
46

moor grass

1800

Lad Gill

↑
45

Low Brown Hill

Mould Gill

Black
Moor

Stonesdale Beck

gate
gate
gate
gate

1700

Frith Lodge

1600

How
Gill   gate ↑
44

1500

to KELD

1400
1300

The path soon levels out as a gate in a wall corner is reached and then contours around Black Moor paralleling Stonesdale Beck and the road to Tan Hill, in underfoot conditions that AW describes as 'very juicy'. After crossing Lad Gill the path, after an initial fairly steep climb, levels out and continues over undulating moorland. Should Lad Gill be unfordable after a period of heavy rain then the road bridge near by can be used. On cresting a slight rise, the Tan Hill Inn is visible in the distance – this has the accolade of being the highest public house in England at 1,732 feet above sea level. On

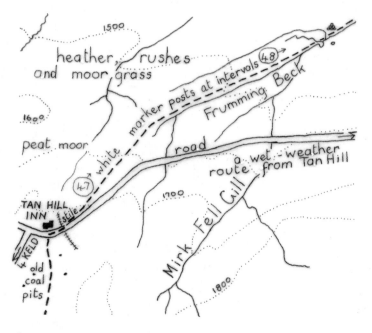

leaving Tan Hill the path continues along the Pennine Way, which is signed by a finger post slightly to the east of the inn. The path is again across moorland, which in this case is, if anything, boggier than that

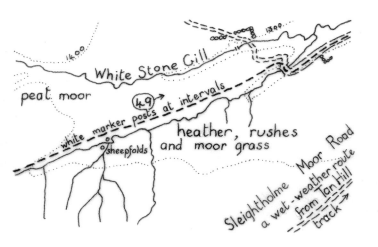

just encountered and for navigation across what is now Sleightholme Moor there are white-tipped marker posts taking the path across the less boggy areas.

In exceptional wet weather conditions take Sleightholme Moor Road, which runs north-east from Tan Hill, for 2¼ miles and then fork left on a track that rejoins the main route short of Sleightholme Farm. After crossing Frumming Beck the path joins a track which passes Sleightholme Farm. Do not take the footbridge opposite the farm but continue to a Pennine Way finger post on the left.

Take the path across fields to a footbridge over Sleightholme Beck by the unexpected escarpment of Bog Scar. Follow the beck initially and then look for signs of a path slanting up to the left to meet a gate in a wall. At Trough Heads the Pennine Way takes alternative routes. One goes north to God's Bridge and across the A66 with the other going to Bowes (the Bowes Loop) – the one taken by the Pennine Journey. The detour to God's Bridge is well worthwhile, as this is a natural phenomenon where plates of rock form a bridge crossing over the River Greta.

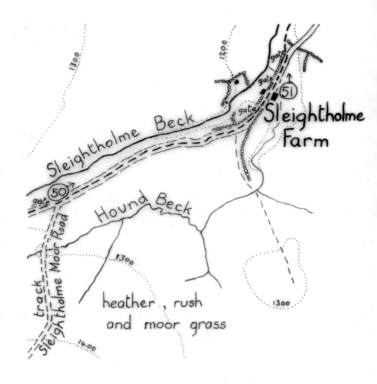

Happily this can now be accommodated due to a newly constructed cinder track following the River Greta downstream through previously inaccessible countryside, to rejoin the main route near East Mellwaters farm. If time (or legs) will not permit the God's Bridge detour, follow the Bowes Loop north. Take care at a junction of tracks by three gates and continue straight on to a farm track, which is then followed to East Mellwaters.

A footbridge is taken over the beck close to its meeting with the River Greta and the path continues through the farmyard of West Charity Farm.

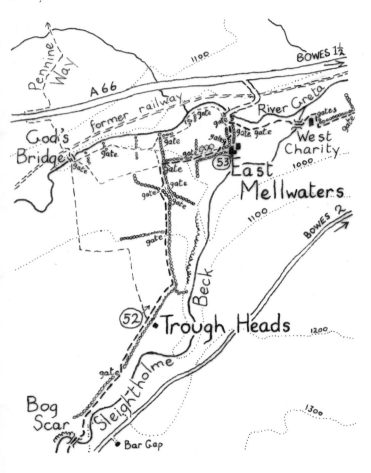

This becomes a lane as it approaches Lady Myres Farm. Soon after the farm, take a path on the left that goes diagonally across a field towards the river and cross on a footbridge by the weir. Follow the river downstream soon taking the obvious grooved track, passing houses which overlook the river, to a stile on the right close to the busy A66. This leads across fields containing the remains of the Roman fort of Lavatris below the castle. A narrow road between the castle and St Giles Church leads into the main street of Bowes.

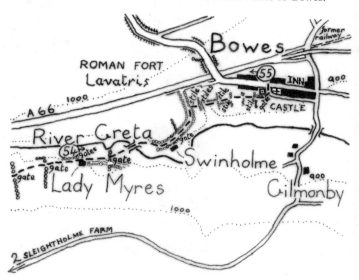

DAY FIVE

Bowes to Middleton-in-Teesdale

Distance	12½ miles
Highest Point	1,417 feet
Height Ascended	1,581 feet
Going	Moderate
Map	O.S. Explorer OL31

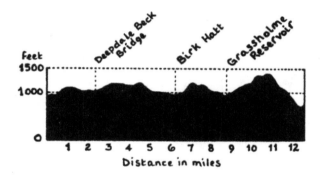

Bowes is a small but strategically placed village on the main pass across the Pennines, and the importance of its position was recognised many years ago. The Romans appreciated its military significance and built their fort and temple of Lavatris here between the second and fourth centuries AD. A millennium later a Norman castle was built on the same site – subsequently strengthened by King Henry II. There is also a famous literary connection. In 1838 Charles Dickens visited Bowes and after learning of the brutal teaching methods used by the proprietor of Bowes Academy immortalised it in his novel *Nicholas Nickleby* under the name of Dotheboys Hall. After leaving the village the path soon rejoins the main Pennine Way route, which is followed for around 10 miles across an area of

Bowes Castle

'sprawling moorland . . . rarely visited by the fraternity of walkers . . . a rolling waste of heather and rushes and rough grass'. Its potential as a source of water supply has been recognised and the path passes close to extensive reservoirs in the Balder and Lune Valleys. There is, however, another literary connection on the path as it passes Low Birk Hatt in the Balder Valley. This is the former home of Hannah Hauxwell, who came to national prominence in the 1980s after being 'discovered' to have run the family farm for over fifty years without the benefit of running water or electricity. She wrote several books about her life and times and retired to the nearby village of Cotherstone (well known for its cheese), through which AW passed on his Pennine Journey.

After passing Kirkcarrion, a hilltop crowned with a copse of trees and with a tumulus reputedly the burial site of a Bronze Age chieftain, there is soon 'a glorious panoramic view of Teesdale, with Middleton, rich in promise of rest and refreshment, directly ahead'.

Kirkcarrion

Route Description

If there wasn't enough time on arriving in Bowes then do make the time before leaving to view this historic town, with its Roman past as well as the ruins of the eleventh-century Norman Keep built on the foundations of Lavatris Roman Fort. Today's walk is entirely on the Pennine Way and so route finding should present no problems. From the castle, walk through the village, noting the many interesting buildings including St Giles' church. After passing Dotheboys Hall, the road swings right over the A66. Follow the road, climbing gradually and from just before a junction there is a magnificent view back to Bowes and its castle. Turn left and follow the road with the 'no through road' sign. After passing the entrance to East Stoney Keld on the right, at the end of the fence and beginning of the wall take the stile (FP sign) on the left. Cross the field diagonally left and make for the outbuildings ahead, looking out for a wall stile. Keep to the right of the barn and head slightly left to another stile in the facing wall.

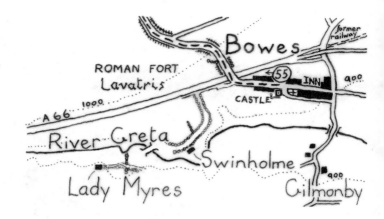

Head straight on keeping left of the broken down fenced off area containing Stoney Keld Spring, with its distinctive stone dome and go left on a slight slope to a large ash tree at a wall corner. Follow the wall to a wooden farm gate and immediately turn right to join a track. Pennine Way signs now point the way past a renovated farm with a thatched roof, where the track bears to the left of the farm and drops down to cross the bridge over Deepdale Beck. At the end of the bridge, go down the steps and continue with the beck on the right, until the path swings left to a marker post with a yellow arrow.

From here, follow white marker posts over the fell on a fairly well defined track crossing Hazelgill Beck. Take a faint track, more or less parallel to the beck below on the right, which heads towards a gateway in the fence ahead. Just before the gate turn left and, keeping to the left of the fence, ascend a faint track to reach a broad track running across the path. Continue straight ahead to follow a narrow track with, initially, a fine stone wall on the right, to reach a metal gate in the facing wall.

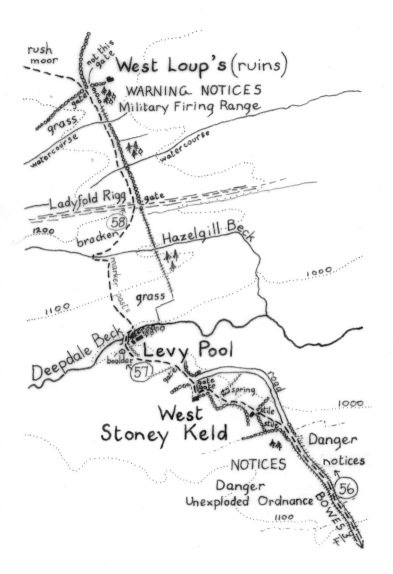

rush moor

not this gate

West Loup's (ruins)

WARNING NOTICES
Military Firing Range

gate

grass

watercourse

watercourse

Ladyfold Rigg

gate

1200

(58)

bracken

Hazelgill Beck

1000

marker posts

grass

1100

Deepdale Beck

boulder

Levy Pool

(57)

gate

gate gate

spring

road

stile

stile

1000

West
Stoney Keld

Danger

notices

(56)

NOTICES
Danger
Unexploded Ordnance

BOWES

1100

Go through and aim diagonally left on a path towards the flat–topped Goldsborough. Ford a stream (there is wooden bridge further on if the beck is swollen) and continue on a clear track keeping Goldsborough on the right. The track finally drops down to reach a metalled road, but if time and energy permit then the diversion to the top of Goldsborough for spectacular views of the three reservoirs of Balderhead, Blackton and Hury, and the fells beyond, is worthwhile. At the road turn left and almost immediately take the farm road to East Friar House. Take care, as it is possible to come down from Goldsborough too far east and reach the road at Mere Beck.

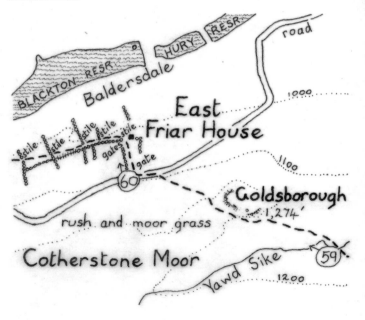

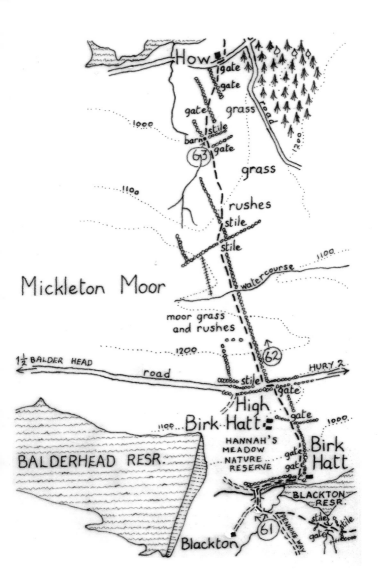

How

gate
gate
gate   grass
stile
barn
gate

63

grass

1000

1100

rushes

stile

stile

watercourse   1100

Mickleton Moor

moor grass
and rushes

1200

62

1½ BALDER HEAD
road   HURY 2

stile
gate

High
Birk Hatt   gate

1100   1000

HANNAH'S
MEADOW   Birk
BALDERHEAD RESR.   NATURE   Hatt
RESERVE   gate
gate

BLACKTON
RESR.

stile
gate   stile

PENNINE WAY

61

Blackton

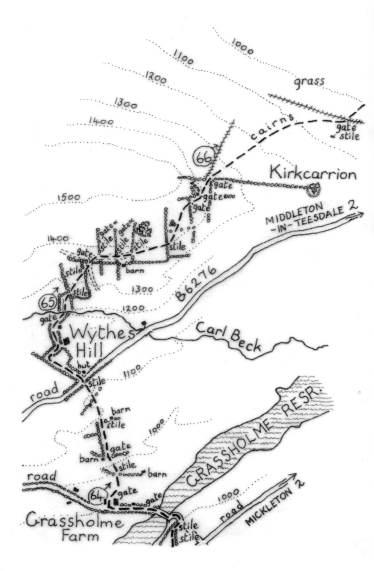

grass

1100

1000

1200

1300

1400

cairns

gate
stile

66

Kirkcarrion

gate
gate
gate

MIDDLETON
-IN-TEESDALE 2

1500

gate
stile

gate
stile

1400

stile

gate
stile

barn

B6276

1300

65

1200

gate

Wythes
Hill

Carl Beck

hut

stile

1100

road

barn
stile

1000

gate

barn

stile

barn

road

64

gate

gate

GRASSHOLME RESR.

1000

Grassholme
Farm

stile
stile

road

MICKLETON 2

From East Friar House, follow Pennine Way signs through fields, using gates and stiles, to arrive on the road above Blackton Bridge. Over the stone bridge bear right to reach Low Birk Hatt through a metal gate and turn left to follow a tarmac track through Hannah's Meadow to reach a road. Turn left briefly, then right at a Pennine Way sign and take the well defined track (the ground can be boggy in places) keeping the stone wall on the right. The path undulates over Mickleton Moor to reach a stile in a facing wall. Over this, bear right to another stile and then left keeping the wall on the left. When the track bears slightly away from the wall, aim for a solitary barn to cross a wall stile next to a wooden gate. Traverse the short field to another wall stile adjacent to the barn. Bear diagonally right over the meadow to reach a metal gate on the right and aim for farm buildings going through two more gates to reach the road close to How. Turn right and then, just after a large ash tree, turn left at a Pennine Way sign. Drop down the field to a cross stile to enter a small copse. Proceed with a wall on the right to reach a squeeze stile in a wall corner. Turn right and, keeping to the right of the wall, arrive on the road at the end of Grassholme Reservoir. Turn left and follow the road down over the bridge and up to Grassholme Farm on the right. Turn right at a Pennine Way sign, cross the farmyard and exit through a metal gate. Follow a well-defined track ascending and descending across five fields to reach a road close to a Nissen hut. Cross the road and take the farm road opposite to Wythes Hill Farm. Just before the farm the track swings left, drops down to pass a cottage on the right and further down enters a short walled lane which leads to a beck. Cross the beck, go through a metal gate and head straight on to reach a stile just before the top right hand corner of the field. Climb diagonally left to a gap in a facing wall and continue in the same direction to cross a wall stile by a metal gate. Turn right on the broad track which continues through four more stiles adjacent to metal gates — after the fourth stile the track bears away left to pass a marker post and cairn.

Cross a rough meadow diagonally to the right to a metal gate and pass a small ruined barn to reach a gate on the left. Follow the path to another gate, bear right and descend the well defined track with cairns assisting the way, to enjoy views of Middleton-in-Teesdale. Across to the right is the tree-topped Kirkcarrion. On reaching a cross fence, take the stile and continue in the same direction down the fell, over the disused railway line and exit through a gate by some houses on to a road. Turn right, then left and follow the main road into Middleton-in-Teesdale and the Bainbridge Memorial, which is on the right upon reaching the T-junction in the town centre.

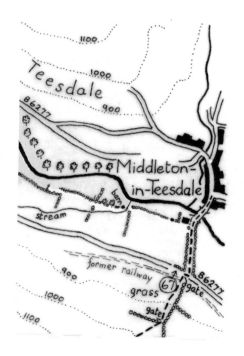

DAY SIX

Middleton-in-Teesdale to Westgate

Distance	15¾ miles
Highest Point	1,991 feet
Height Ascended	2,306 feet
Going	Moderate with one steep climb
Map	O.S. Explorer OL31

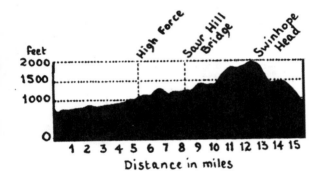

Middleton, the 'capital' of Upper Teesdale, is a small market town but is yet another community on the journey with links to the lead mining industry. In fact, it owes its present size, and its many fine Victorian buildings, to a decision by the London Lead Company in the early nineteenth century to move its headquarters in the north of England to here from Blanchland in Northumberland. Today's starting point – the 1877 Bainbridge Memorial – is named after a former Company superintendent. Ironically tomorrow's stage will end in Blanchland.

The path today is a varied one and starts with an 8-mile stretch of the Pennine Way by the River Tees that is quite memorable. AW put it perfectly in his *Pennine Way Companion* when he said it was 'a joy to the naturalist, the geologist and the botanist; and to the walker who has tramped . . . bleak moors.' It is particularly rewarding in early summer, when the banks of the Tees and the meadows 'are ablaze with flowers'. One feature of the route along the River Tees is the bridges that cross the river and the route passes five — the first three being footbridges.

Scoberry Bridge

The most significant one though is the Wynch Bridge, the first ever suspension bridge. The present one dates from 1830 but this replaced one from 1704 that was built for lead miners to get across the river. The other striking features of this stretch are the waterfalls of Low Force and the more dramatic one of High Force where the river plunges 70 feet. The short walk along the Tees is eastward, but the journey since Settle so far has been essentially northbound and it is this general direction which must be resumed for the next destination — Westgate in Weardale. Footpaths lead out of the valley until Swinhope Head is reached. At 1992 feet, it was AW's 'highest point northwards'. Here his 1938 route is taken for the remaining 3½ miles of this stage — sadly not on the green road that he enjoyed after taking a 'beguiling short cut', where he 'was soon floundering knee-deep in slimy peat'.

High Force

Route Description

From the Bainbridge Memorial drinking fountain walk down Bridge Street over the road bridge across the River Tees and take the footpath to the right (PW). The route along the river is mainly level, easy to follow and in most places is immediately by the Tees, except when it veers slightly away to the south. Under normal walking conditions it is all dry underfoot, or paved or boarded, and for 8 miles follows the Pennine Way, clearly signposted. There are short uphill sections but none is particularly long or tiring. The path passes Scoberry Bridge, followed shortly by Wynch Bridge (from where there is a delightful view of Low Force) and lastly Holwick Head Bridge. Do not cross, but fork half left up the man-made steps. At the top go through a kissing gate to enter the Upper Teesdale National Nature Reserve.

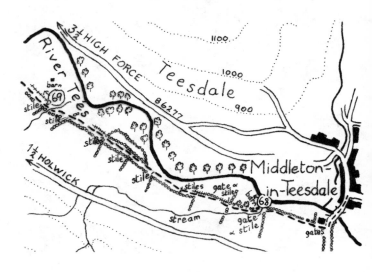

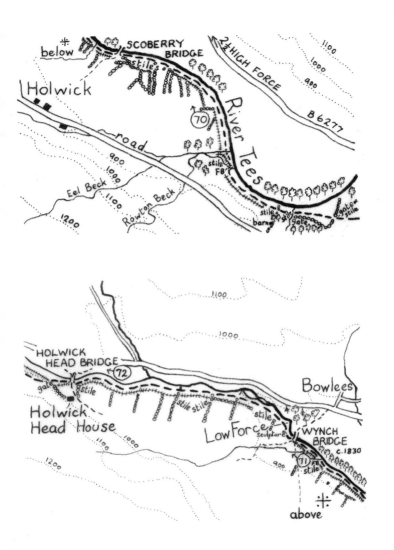

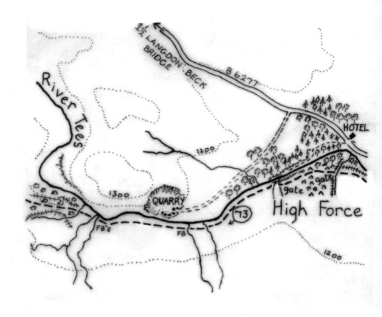

Follow the surfaced path and, just before reaching High Force, note a short track to the right, which provides a spectacular view of one of England's largest waterfalls, where the Tees plunges 70 feet into an amphitheatre of sheer-sided Whin Sill. After crossing three footbridges there is an uphill section between boulders and junipers to pass a corrugated barn (a covered railway wagon). Aim for two small stone posts on top of Bracken Rigg and take the direction shown by the right hand one (PW) downhill to a stile. A paved footpath goes uphill then downhill and finally concludes at a gated wall stile on the right. Cross over and turn left on a short but steep descent to another stile. The path leads to a gate beside a barn at Cronkley Farm, turns left and follows a wide farm track down to Cronkley Bridge. After crossing over the bridge, turn left (SP PW) and follow the river upstream. This section passes the confluence of Langdon Beck and the

Tees, and may be impassable in flood conditions (*in which case take the farm track from Cronkley Bridge to join the B6277*). Follow the riverside path to reach Saur Hill Bridge — here the Pennine Journey leaves the Pennine Way and does not rejoin it until Hadrian's Wall. Do not cross the bridge but turn right along a farm track until it splits. At this junction keep straight on by the right hand side of the wall, go over a stile at the corner of a cross wall and continue to a gate in the field wall. Once through the gate turn right and aim for a gate to the left hand side of the farm ahead. Follow the farm track to the B6277.

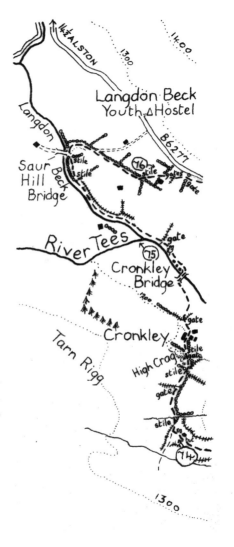

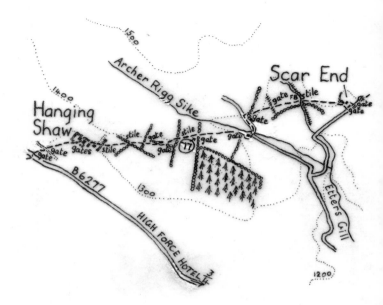

Take the gate opposite and go uphill half right to a gate by a white house to cross an enclosed lane. Once through the facing gate, cross the field towards a deserted house (Hanging Shaw), partially hidden behind trees. Take the gate on the right, bear right over the stream, enter the farmyard and go past the farmhouse. Aim for a ladder stile ahead and go through the gate immediately on the left. Pass a barn and head uphill to another ladder stile in the top corner of the next field. Cross and walk half right to a metal gate, then keep to the left hand wall to reach derelict farm buildings. There are green markers next to the gate across the path. Go straight ahead to a wall stile. Bear diagonally left to another stile and aim for a black corrugated barn, going through a gate and crossing a small stone bridge en route. Immediately after the barn, turn sharp left and head for a gate in a wall. Go through and cross the field keeping to the left of a ruined hut. Continue close to the right hand wall and descend to a footbridge and stile.

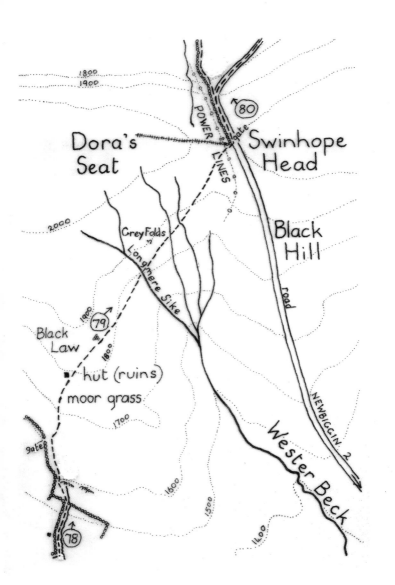

1800
1900

Dora's
Seat

POWER LINES

gate

80

Swinhope
Head

2000

Grey Folds

Longmere Sike

Black
Hill

road

1900

79

1800

Black
Law

hut (ruins)

moor grass

1700

1600

1500

NEWBIGGIN. 2

Wester Beck

1400

gate

78

Follow the wall uphill and, where it bears right, continue straight on towards Scar End. At the farm take the gate in the facing wall onto the farm lane. Turn left and go through a gate where the track leads down to a wooden bridge over a stream. Climb slightly and go through the left hand of two gates and walk uphill between the wall and beck. Keep close to the wall and pass through two kissing gates. Aim diagonally left to meet a wall at a depression in the ridge ahead and follow a faint track for about 250 yards to a wooden gate in the wall. Here leave the wall, heading diagonally right to climb gradually over the moorland with no distinct path to follow. After about 300 yards a ruined shooting hut of stone and rusty red corrugated sheeting is reached. At this point two tracks come in from the right. Do not turn directly right, but take the fairly well defined track half right around the shoulder of the hillock.

On the stretch from here to Swinhope Head there is, for those anxious to keep their feet relatively dry, ample opportunity to practice the dying skill of tussock hopping. After 100 yards, on a clear day, a line of telegraph poles reaching to the skyline can be seen ahead. The last of these (a double post) is a guide to the road at Swinhope Head. Half way between this point and the road, there is a derelict sheepfold. Aim for this over boggy moorland with no distinct path. En route to the sheepfold cross two or three gullies, the last of which is quite deep and here a slight diversion upstream may be needed in order to cross. Continue over very rough moorland terrain to meet the road just beyond the double telegraph post. In mist, without the benefit of the guiding telegraph poles, head east to pick up the Westgate – Newbiggin road. The route ahead is now simple – following, mostly, the road into Westgate. Where the road swings away from the wall the path descends steeply. In wet conditions continue round the loop in the road – the extra distance is negligible.

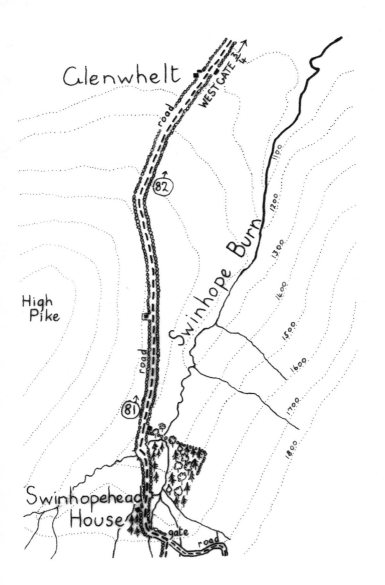

Glenwhelt

WESTGATE 3

road

82

Swinhope Burn

High
Pike

road

1100
1200
1300
1400
1500
1600
1700
1800

81

Swinhopehead
House

gate

road

The route has now reached Weardale. Cross over a minor road to a ford and adjacent footbridge over the River Wear. Turn right on the A689 into the village, where the Hare and Hounds awaits thirsty walkers.

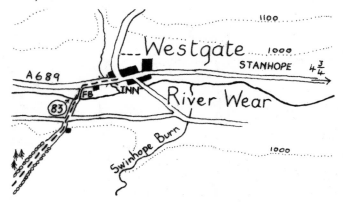

DAY SEVEN

Westgate to Blanchland

Distance	10¾ miles
Highest Point	1,692 feet
Height Ascended	1,522 feet
Going	Moderate with one steep climb
Map	O.S. Explorer 307

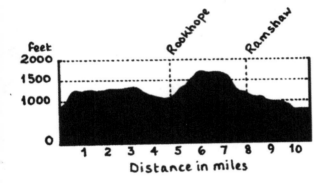

Weardale lies at the heart of what has become known as England's last wilderness – a comparatively unknown expanse of hills, moorland and hidden valleys in the Northern Pennines – parts of which have been traversed in the past two stages. The twentieth-century poet W.H. Auden wrote: 'My great good place is the part of the Pennines bounded on the S by Swaledale, on the N by the Roman wall and on the W by the Eden Valley,' and he featured the area in many of his works.

On leaving Weardale it is interesting to reflect that the river crossed by the footbridge yesterday had at its mouth, when AW crossed it in 1938, one of England's principal shipbuilding centres. It should also come as no surprise to learn that this area was another major centre of the lead mining industry. But it was not just a lead mining area,

River Wear, Westgate

as Westgate was the Weardale Iron Company's railhead for ironstone from Wearhead and Ireshopeburn.

Westgate is left on another long distance footpath – the Weardale Way, which traces the river from its beginning at Wearhead to its mouth at Sunderland. On its way it passes the magnificent Durham Cathedral and Auckland Castle – the seat of the Prince Bishops of Durham. Westgate and neighbouring Eastgate derive their names from gates into the mediaeval hunting park of the castle. The journey passes through Rookhope in an area full of industrial archaeology but which 500 years ago was notorious for border reiving.

The path here joins another coast-to-coast route – the Sustrans C2C cycle path – as it makes its way up Bolt's Law Incline. This is famous among railway historians for being a track with a standing engine at the top which pulled the trains up the incline and was instrumental in the line reaching a height of 1,670 feet, the highest point achieved by a standard gauge line in Britain. The hill of Bolt's

Law has been dominant throughout the day and from there the path drops down to Ramshaw for the start of two delightful riverside walks. The first is along Bolt's Burn to Baybridge where the River Derwent is joined for the final stroll into Blanchland.

Rookhope

Route Description

From the Hare and Hounds, take the minor road almost directly opposite which heads north and uphill out of the village to Scarsike Head to join the route of the Weardale Way – the seventh long distance footpath encountered since setting out on the Pennine Journey. Ignore a finger post (SP Weardale Way) just before the road steepens but when it takes a very sharp left hand bend, a metal footpath sign indicates the way on the right. Take the lane which becomes a hardcore farm road and then an easy grass path with occasional Weardale Way waymarkers. On approaching Heights Quarry, a clear track can be seen ahead on the old tramway. The path disappears if followed straight ahead – on crossing a stile, drop down on the left through a

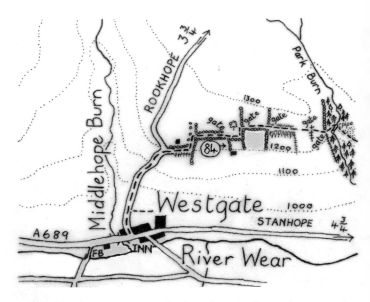

copse of larch trees to cross a beck and regain the track among signs of mineral workings.

The path soon reaches Heights Quarry and skirts round its southern edge. This is a working quarry and quite busy during the week so take care to follow any posted instructions – the footpath has been diverted slightly. After a short section of fenced path, cross the quarry road and continue straight ahead through a gate. The path continues around the edge of the quarry on an old track, and when this goes through cuttings (which can be wet), take to the embankments. After passing two small plantations the track swings north and then north-east before descending via Smailsburn into Rookhope.

On reaching Rookhope, cross the bridge over the Rookhope Burn and turn right on the road to the Rookhope Inn. The climb up to Bolt's Law uses the Sustrans C2C cycle path opposite the Post Office. It is a steady pull up the Bolt's Law Incline with some 600 feet of

1500

Smailsburn

Deep Cleugh

gate
gate
87

Bishop Seat

High
Bishop Seat

Crow's Cleugh

gate

Lapwing

stile
gate
old railway
cutting

embankment
86

1100

1400

hurdle

1300

stile

Heights
Quarry

stile
stile hurdle

1200

gate

gate 85

RS

Rookhope Burn
Rookhope

gate

gate

gates

gate

ascent in a little over a mile before it levels out and continues on to a large sheepfold on the right hand side of the track. *To take in the summit of Bolt's Law there are two alternatives. From the sheepfold go uphill through the heather heading for what appears to be a gate in the fence. Here two wire fences meet and the summit cairn is visible ahead. A more defined route is from the marker post mentioned below. From here a track on the left leads uphill past another marker post to a gate close to the trig point and cairn.* At the sheepfold, where the track swings away to the right, head for the fence and locate a prominent stile by a post. From here a faint path leads to a marker post at a junction of paths. At the marker post a solitary tree is in sight on the right – the tree is decorated with sweets every December by a local running club that uses these moorland paths for training. Head towards the tree and just before it is reached take a path heading north. Two chimneys are in view: head for the more westerly of the two. Paths run either side of the chimney down to Ramshaw but the route takes the one to the west. At a kissing gate on the left the path drops down to a footbridge then on to a gate on the right.

Head away from the fence and drop downhill on a well defined path towards reclaimed mine workings. Turn right by a derelict building and follow the old mine road to where it joins the road at Ramshaw. At a fork in the road turn right, ignore the next two wooden signposts and at a metal signpost on the left take the track down towards Bolt's Burn. Look out for a waymarked path on the right which is followed through the wood with Bolt's Burn below.

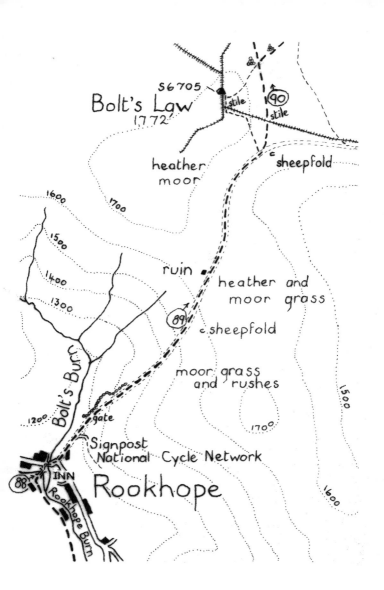

Bolt's Law
1,772'

S6705

stile

90

stile

heather
moor

sheepfold

1600

1700

1500

1400

1300

ruin

heather and
moor grass

89

c.sheepfold

moor grass
and rushes

Bolt's Burn

1500

1200

gate

1700

Signpost
National Cycle Network

88

INN

Rookhope

Rookhope Burn

1600

1600

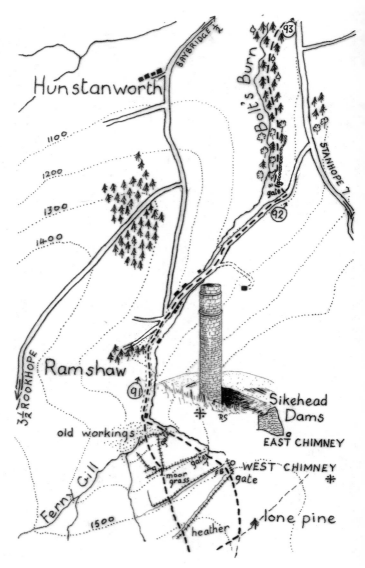

Hunstanworth

BAYBRIDGE 2

Bolt's Burn

93

STANHOPE 7

1100

1200

1300

1400

92

gate

3¾ ROOKHOPE

Ramshaw

91

RS

Sikehead
Dams

EAST CHIMNEY

old workings

gate

gate

WEST CHIMNEY

Ferny Gill

moor
grass

gate

1500

heather

lone pine

A broad forest track is met which leads to a gate on to the road to Baybridge. Turn left down to the bridge over the River Derwent and, before crossing the bridge, take a footpath on the right that accompanies the river all the way into Blanchland. This picturesque village with its fine stone buildings will well repay the time spent exploring it. In 1938 AW thought 'the medieval atmosphere of Blanchland was something to marvel at' and, 70 years later, it still is.

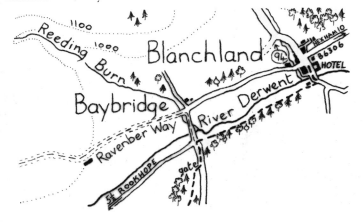

DAY EIGHT

Blanchland to Hexham

Distance	11¾ miles
Highest Point	1,289 feet
Height Ascended	1,230 feet
Going	Moderate with two steep climbs
Map	O.S. Explorer 307 & OL43

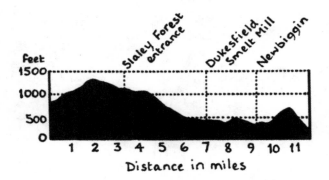

AW said that 'when you set foot in Blanchland, you step into the Middle Ages' – a romantic evening vision that did not stand up to his daytime scrutiny. It is though, without doubt, one of the most attractive villages that the Pennine Journey encounters. An abbey of the Premonstratensian order was built here in the early thirteenth century, and while it survived many a border raid it could not survive Dissolution under Henry VIII. Eventually it passed into the hands of Lord Crewe, a Bishop of Durham in the mid-seventeenth century – part of the building is contained in the well-appointed hostelry, the Lord Crewe Arms. The impressive medieval gatehouse that accommodates the post office (with a rare Victorian post box) and shop is another reminder of Blanchland's monastic past.

Blanchland

Industry has also played its part in Blanchland's history. Lead had been mined here for many years and it was the discovery of better seams a little further south that prompted the move of the London Lead Company's offices to Middleton-in-Teesdale. This stage links the site of a forgotten abbey with that of a living abbey at Hexham.

Dukesfield Smelt Mill

The route crosses Blanchland Moor before entering Slaley Forest – when AW passed this way the trees were 'only a few feet high' – and then accompanies Devil's Water, with the remains of Dukesfield Smelt Mill nearby.

The path passes through fields with the town of Hexham and the tower of the abbey coming increasingly into view. As this is a relatively short stage there should be time to look around the magnificent abbey which contains many noteworthy historical objects.

Route Description

From the crossroads leave the village on the 'no through road', passing the tea room on the right and the free car park on the left. The road winds uphill through a wooded glen until the houses of the old lead mining community of Shildon are reached. Here the road becomes a track which is followed, ignoring the finger post on the right, to Pennypie House, formerly an old coaching inn on the drove road between Hexham and Blanchland. Through the gate the track bends to the right climbing to another gate. Make sure to turn and admire the views across the Derwent Valley and at the next gate look to the east to see part of the huge Derwent Reservoir. Ignore a track on the left and head for a gate at the edge of Slaley Forest. Through the gate take the left hand fork, ignore the next left, go past the entrance to Ladycross Quarry and soon take a straight, wide track on the left. This is currently being extended through the forest to a junction of byways. Continue ahead to meet a tarmac road and follow it downhill.

Where the road turns left at a right angle, turn right and follow the bridleway. Soon, at a fork, take the track going off left and follow this through the wood, with Devil's Water down below, to pass Redlead Mill house. Just past the house the woodland opens up to create a suitable lunch spot at a ruined building by the stream. The track keeps to the right of the river and after passing the third bridge over Devil's Water soon arrives at the two well-preserved gothic arches

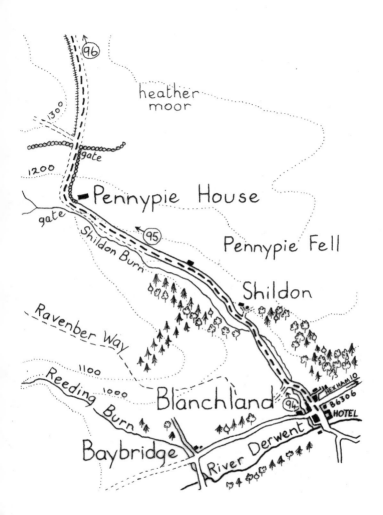

heather
moor

1300

1200

gate

96

gate

Pennypie House

95

Shildon Burn

Pennypie Fell

Shildon

Ravenber Way

1100

1000

Reeding Burn

Blanchland

94

HEXHAM 10

B6306

HOTEL

Baybridge

River Derwent

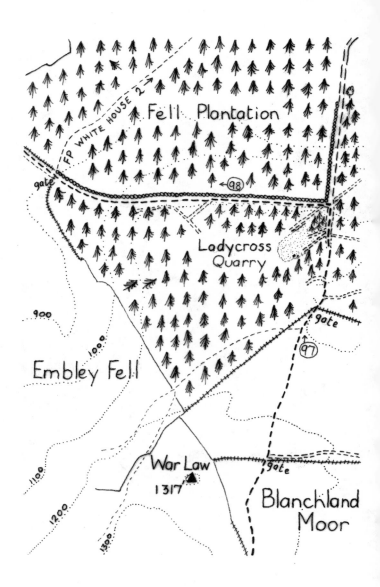

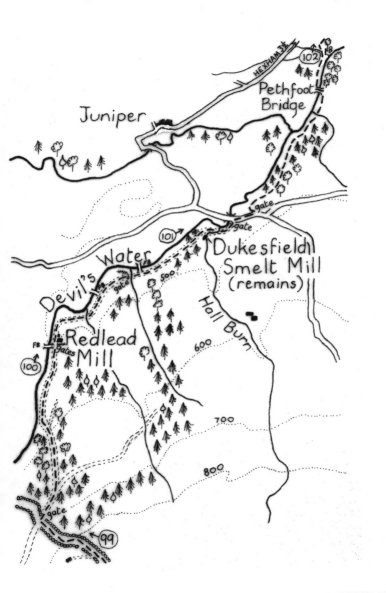

Juniper

Pethfoot
Bridge

HEXHAM 3½

102

FB

Water

Devil's

101

Dukesfield
Smelt Mill
(remains)

gate

gate

500

Hall Burn

600

Redlead
Mill

FB

gates

100

700

800

gate

99

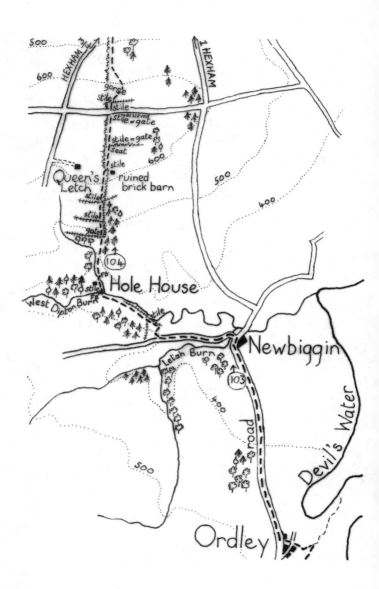

500

600

HEXHAM

1 HEXHAM

gorse
stile
stile
stile or gate
RESERVOIR
stile or gate
seat
stile

600

500

400

Queen's
Letch

ruined
brick barn

stiles

stile

gates

104

Hole House

West Dipton Burn

stile

stile

Newbiggin

Letah Burn

103

400

500

road

Devil's Water

Ordley

of Dukesfield smelt mill. This seventeenth-century mill was built on the Dukesfield estate and used to smelt lead ore until 1834 when the process was transferred to the mills of Allendale and Rookhope. The track ends at a gate by the road: turn right and almost immediately look for a half-hidden signpost (Pethfoot Bridge ¾m) on the left hand side of the road. Follow the track through the wood crossing a tributary to reach Pethfoot Bridge. Cross and turn right along a pleasant riverside path to a footbridge, reached over log steps.

Take the left hand path and walk uphill to reach a track. Here turn left to reach a small estate of attractive houses at Ordley. The path is to the left of the house opposite emerging on to the road; turn right and continue to the bridge. Take the minor road left over the bridge, passing an entrance to the National Trust's Letah Wood. Take a stile on the right (FP Hexham 2¼m/Dipton Mill ¾m), zigzag down the hillside under the telegraph wires and go left along the line of poles to a stile. Follow the stream to a footbridge and take the path towards Hole House, ignoring the 'Path Legally Diverted' sign. Look

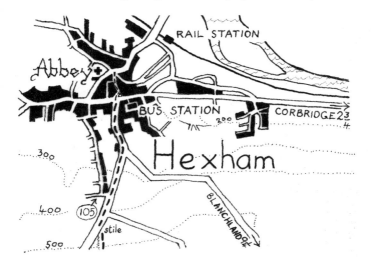

for a gate in the corner of the property, cross another bridge and go uphill through the woods to a gate. Continue straight ahead taking a stile after a ruined brick building on the right. Now walk with the hedge on the left and pause to take in the views from the convenient seat dedicated to a stalwart of Hexham Ramblers group. At the next stile by a grassed reservoir a minor road is reached. Use the ladder stile opposite and drop steeply down the field with good views of Hexham. The path stays in a straight line through gorse bushes to a stile in the corner to meet a road. Turn right and follow the road downhill into Hexham to arrive at a busy junction. Use one of the 'wynds' – narrow alleyways – to gain access to the main market area and the abbey.

DAY NINE

Hexham to Housesteads

Distance	15½ miles
Highest Point	1,050 feet
Height Ascended	2,175 feet
Going	Moderate with two climbs
Map	O.S. Explorer OL43

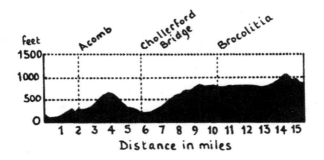

Hexham is the first real town on the Pennine Journey since Settle and it is a very historic one. Despite its close proximity to Hadrian's Wall and its associated forts there is no specific Roman connection. However, stones from the nearby fort of Corstopitum at Corbridge were used in the construction of the seventh-century Benedictine abbey, which, 500 years later, was replaced by an Augustinian priory but the original Saxon crypt survives. Other attractions in the town are the Moot Hall and the Old Gaol (now a museum) – reputedly the oldest purpose built gaol in the country. Just west of the town is the confluence of the North Tyne and the South Tyne, and on reaching the late-eighteenth-century stone bridge over the Tyne it is obvious one of England's principal rivers is about to be crossed. The architect and engineer of the bridge, Robert Mylne,

Hexham Abbey

also designed Chollerford Bridge over the North Tyne which will be crossed later today.

The route is heading towards, and is now close to, the main objective of AW's journey – Hadrian's Wall. This has the unique distinction of being a World Heritage Site and also a National Trail. The authorities have recognised that satisfying their responsibilities for both these aspects is, at times, contradictory. Put simply, overuse of that part of the National Trail where the archaeology is most at risk would damage the World Heritage Site. Ironically, on page 68 of his *Pennine Way Companion* AW discusses 'Conservation versus Destruction' – albeit in respect of the possible flooding of part of the Upper Tees Valley to make a reservoir. The current answer is to encourage the use of the Hadrian's Wall Path as a spring/summer/autumn route. In co-operation with the authorities, Mark Richards has written *The Roman Ring*, and it is hoped that responsible walkers will use the southern part of this walk during the winter months.

Planetrees

Our first view of the Wall is at Planetrees and then in fairly quick succession comes Chollerford where the Romans bridged the North Tyne and Cilurnum Fort (Chesters). For AW in 1938, his arrival here was the high point of his journey and he spent some time being transported back in time to the days when it was an active and busy fort. At nearby Walwick the vallum and ditch are encountered for the first time with, intermittently, small sections of the Wall – all three running parallel to each other and 'absolutely in a straight line'. After rounding Limestone Corner, the Wall's most northerly point, Brocolitia Fort with its Mithraic temple is reached and soon the road, which has been shadowing the path for some miles, is left. The road, one of General Wade's mid-eighteenth-century military roads, used the Wall as its foundation. The stage comes to a dramatic conclusion as the path traverses the rim of Sewingshields Crags with great views of Broomlee Lough and, as it is approached, ever improving views of the magnificent ruins of Vircovicium Fort (Housesteads).

Route Description

From the Market Place, walk towards the Forum Cinema and descend Hallstile Bank. Pass by the mini-roundabout with Haugh Lane and continue along Alemouth Road, with the Car and Coach Park on the right. Keep straight on at the next roundabout with Station Road and carry on to cross the railway and the bridge over the River Tyne. *For those who choose to respect the wishes of the National Trail authorities and avoid Hadrian's Wall in the 'off season' between 1 November and 30 April then the recommended alternative route — see the beginning of this chapter for more information — starts by taking the road to Tyne Green Country Park on the left just before crossing the bridge over the river. Details of where this alternative route rejoins the main route can be found in Day 11.* Once over the bridge, take the next turning to the left (SP St John Lee Bridge) and cross over the A69. Turn right and then left up the lane to reach an intersection. Take the second road on the left and, after passing some attractive estate cottages and an entrance to Riding Farm, proceed straight ahead along a bridleway with a view of Acomb village. Cross the stream over a stone bridge, continue the gentle ascent and enter a little square with a stone block fountain and a cast iron tub. From the village square, turn left down the main street to a footpath sign on the right at the Sun Inn. Keep to the right and walk straight on. Descend many steps to cross a stream on a footbridge. Bear right, and follow the field boundary and a stone wall to a ladder stile. Turn left towards Halfway House, and then right at the minor road. The way ascends gradually passing through the farm buildings at Fallowfield.

At the top of the slope keep straight on through the gateway to Crag House for a few paces. Head for a gate on the right and walk slightly left round a paddock boundary following a power line. Descend the field slope and look ahead to the left to get the first view of a section of Hadrian's Wall at Planetrees. Aim for two wooden stables, cross an adjacent stile and over the lane is a signpost indicating the close proximity of Hadrian's Wall. Follow the hedge

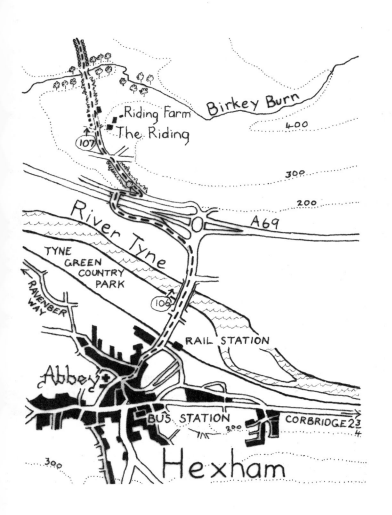

down the field to a step stile and strike out across the pasture to arrive at the Wall. From here the route follows the Hadrian's Wall Path National Trail opened in 2003, which traces the Roman frontier from Wallsend to Bowness-on-Solway, a distance of 84 miles. Aim for the west end of the Wall section to a ladder stile and walk down the meadow to a similar stile. Proceed through a strip of woodland to reach a minor road. The Hadrian's Wall route bears left here to meet the A6079 which is followed right to Low Brunton crossroads. On the right, just before the crossroads, are the remains of Brunton Turret. Turn left to Chollerford Bridge. For those with time available (or an interest in Roman history) take a gate on the left before the bridge and follow the footpath leading downstream to inspect the remains of the Roman bridge. Return to and cross over the bridge, passing the George Hotel, and go left along the B6318 using the footpath on the right hand side of the road. The entrance to the Roman fort of Chesters soon appears on the left and, once more if time permits, take the opportunity to explore the ruins and visit the museum. Otherwise, it's quick march up the hill to Walwick after passing Chesters Stud, an imposing edifice complete with clock tower. Turn right along the signposted lane at Walwick and take the ladder stile on the left. Follow a line of small hawthorn trees to reach a step stile and then a series of ladder stiles en route to the minor road at Tower Tye. Turn right, and then pass through a gap stile on the left. The path is laid with chippings and then slabs as it winds round a wooded area.

A step stile stands on the north Ditch of Hadrian's Wall. Walk through the Ditch to a small gate, bear right keeping above the earthworks of Milecastle 29, and follow the roadside wall to a kissing gate. Cross the lane, leading to the farm at Black Carts, to a similar gate. The path passes a fine section of consolidated Wall including Turret 29a and soon after, a further stretch of consolidated Wall is met, as the ground ascends. The path climbs

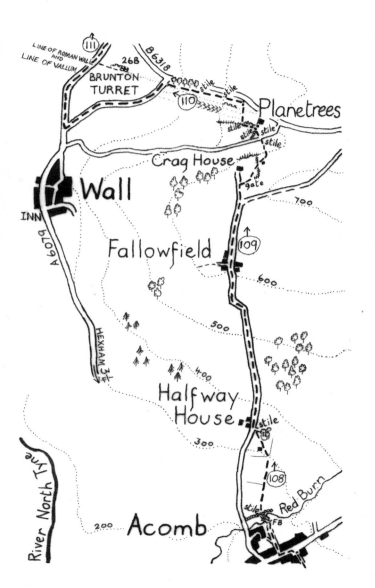

Line of Roman Wall AND Line of Vallum

111

B6318

268

BRUNTON TURRET

110

stile

stile

Planetrees

stile stile

stile

Crag House

stile

gate

700

Wall

INN

A6079

Fallowfield

109

600

500

HEXHAM 3½

400

Halfway House

stile

300

108

Red Burn

stile

River North Tyne

200

Acomb

FB

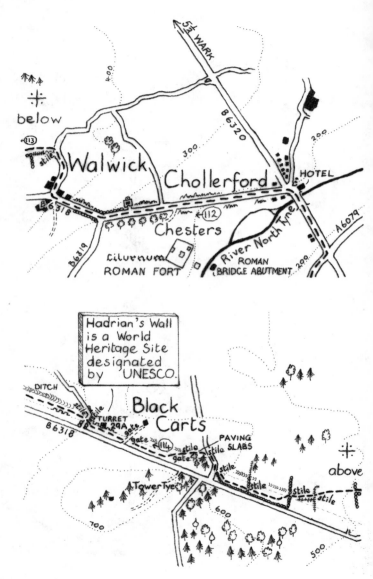

Hadrian's Wall is a World Heritage Site designated by UNESCO.

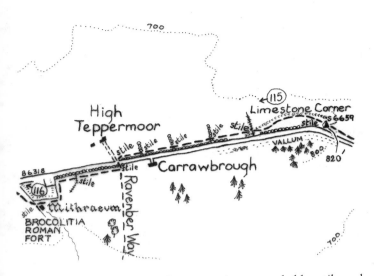

to meet a redundant O.S. column, continues to a ladder stile and accompanies the shallow north Ditch to reach a section of tumbled boulders known as Limestone Corner — the most northerly point of Hadrian's Wall where on a clear day there are extensive views to the uplands around Redesdale and the Simonside Hills with the outlines of the Cheviots in the distance. The path now crosses through the north Ditch and after several stiles arrives at the track to High Teppermoor. Bear left, cross over the main road to steps down into the field and follow the roadside wall to the car park at Brocolitia Roman Fort. *For a hundred yards or so on either side of the car park the route is shared with that of the Ravenber Way — an alternative coast-to-coast path devised by Ron Scholes who has drawn the route maps for this guide book.*

Take the well-used path from the car park to the temple of Mithras and from there a flagged path to a ladder stile then across more slabs through the marshy area of Meggie's Dene Burn. This rush covered boggy location was once the site of the shrine of the

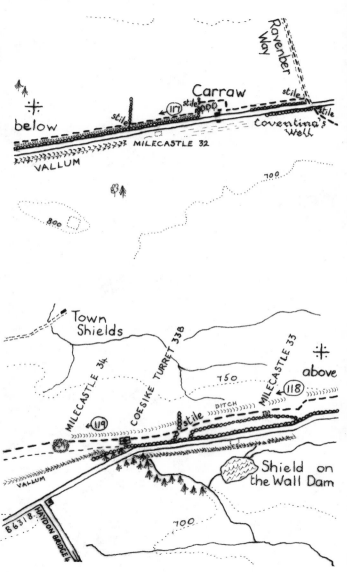

goddess Coventina. An enormous quantity of Roman coins, carved stones and other votive offerings were found when the well was excavated. The path crosses the main road via stiles and proceeds up the pasture, climbing gently to Carraw with its farm and clump of trees. There are slabs to negotiate to reach a step stile. Bear left and follow the roadside wall to reach a ladder stile and continue on the right hand of the north Ditch which becomes more prominent. Directly ahead, the wood and scarp of Sewingshields become distinctly visible.

Use the stone steps to cross to the left hand side of the north Ditch to approach the remains of Milecastle 33 and its wooden viewing platform. The walking is now along a low rubble bank which contains the remains of the Wall and is straightforward. Pass by a single-storey stone cottage and cross the rough farm track to a small gate into Sewingshields Wood. Walk past farm buildings and leave the wood by another small gate. This is a fine part of the walk along the crest of the crags. The Wall masonry disappears, only to reappear in short sections and soon another O.S. column is reached with a splendid view of Broomlee Lough. Follow the field wall down the scarp edge to a small gate in the gap named King's Wicket – a reference to King Arthur. Continue on over King's Hill,

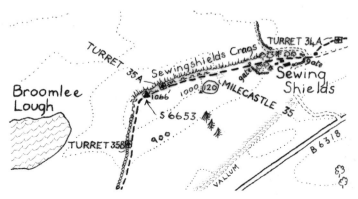

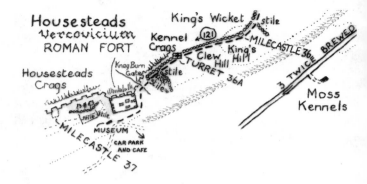

with its neat field wall, down into the next dip, and ascend Clew
Hill. Descend sharply, climb up to Kennel Crags with its coppice of
mixed woodland and head for a ladder stile. Leave the wood at a step
stile in a wall corner with an impressive section of reconstructed
Roman wall. Descend to Knag Burn Gate, a rare form of gateway
through the wall inserted in the fourth century, and climb the rising
ground towards the east gate of Housesteads Roman Fort. Go left
around the fort to the English Heritage reception and museum.

DAY TEN

Housesteads to Greenhead

Distance	9¾ miles
Highest Point	1,112 feet
Height Ascended	1,526 feet
Going	Moderate
Map	O.S. Explorer OL43

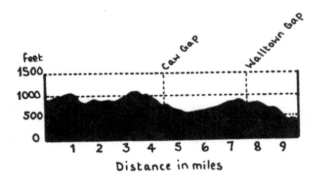

For virtually the whole of this day the path is along the Hadrian's Wall National Trail, route finding is straightforward and the stage, at just less than 10 miles, is a relatively short one. So if Chesters Fort was not visited yesterday, there is ample time to get an appreciation of the history that underpins this section of the Pennine Journey by visiting the museum and exploring the substantial remains of the Roman fort of Vircovicium (Housesteads).

Certainly the entrance fee to the fort, owned by the National Trust but managed and maintained by English Heritage, is good value for money. AW described his arrival at Housesteads as being 'at last at the foot of the rainbow, at the end of my quest'. Here his imagination ran riot.

Housesteads

On the route, a backward look from Cuddy's Crags provides a classic picture of Housesteads Crags and at the nearby Rapishaw Gap the Pennine Way is met again as it heads north, with still over 50 miles to go to its destination at Kirk Yetholm.

Cuddy's Crags

On the descent from Hotbank Crags there is a glorious view of Crag Lough below the formidable Highshield Crags. At Sycamore Gap (which has acquired sufficient notoriety since it featured in the film *Robin Hood: Prince of Thieves* to have been given the nickname of Robin Hood's Gap) there is the large tree that gives this dip its name. Hopefully this name will continue, as its successor is already 'in the wings' waiting to take over.

The Wall in this stretch is particularly impressive and much of this is due to the zeal of John Clayton, owner of the Chester estate. In the nineteenth century he devoted a considerable amount of time and money to preserving much of it. The ups and downs together with the succession of milecastles and turrets, to say nothing of the splendid views heading westwards, make for an airy walk.

On Windshields Crags an O.S. column, at 1,132 feet, marks the high point of the National Trail, and within the next 5 miles are two quarries, Cawfield and Walltown, which destroyed parts of the Wall. Quarrying ceased many years ago and the quarries have now been landscaped with visitor facilities. The path, as it drops down into Greenhead, passes close to the ruins of the fourteenth-century Thirlwall Castle built mainly of stone from the Wall and restored recently by Northumberland County Council.

Route Description

Pick up the route at the north-west corner of the fort where it is permitted to follow the Wall by the simple expedient of walking on its reinforced top, through the pines of Housesteads Wood, as it heads west away from the fort. This short section ends at a gate out of the wood and the path leads on to Milecastle 37, with its distinctive partial archway in the North Gate. At Cuddy's Crags there is a classic view of Housesteads Crags before dropping down into Rapishaw Gap. Here a ladder stile on the right takes the Pennine Way away from the Wall on its northbound journey to Wark Forest and the Cheviots. Cross another ladder stile and follow the Wall as it goes along Hotbank Crags and then descends past Hotbank Farm, from where there is a magnificent view of Crag Lough below Windshields Crags.

The Wall turns to the right and over the next ladder stile is Milking Gap. Cross a farm access track, go over a stile and follow the footpath with the field wall on the left to a ladder stile into the wood skirting Crag Lough. Leaving Crag Lough behind, a stile is encountered where the Wall reappears. Sycamore Gap, the halfway point on this Pennine Journey, has a steep descent and ascent and is soon followed by Milecastle 39 and the impressive Peel Crags.

Soon the road by the car park at Steel Rigg is reached and from here the path rises to the O.S. column on Windshields Crags. There are more steep ascents and descents passing Milecastle 41 and Bogle Hole to reach the road at Caw Gap. A pair of kissing gates leads to a fine section

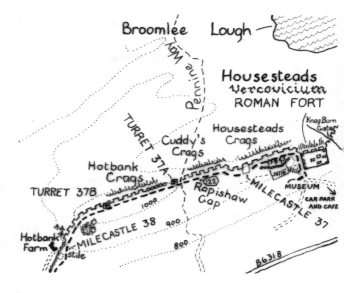

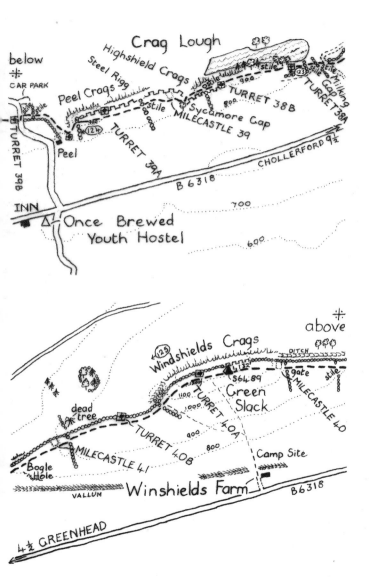

below

CAR PARK

TURRET 39B

INN

Peel Crags

Steel Rigg

Highshield Crags

Crag Lough

stile

TURRET 38B

123

Milking Gap

TURRET 38A

stile

Peel

TURRET 39A

124

stile

MILECASTLE 39

Sycamore Gap

900

800

CHOLLERFORD 9½

B 6318

700

600

Once Brewed
Youth Hostel

above

Windshields Crags

125

DITCH

gate

stile

126

864.89

MILECASTLE 40

Green
Slack

TURRET 40A

1100

1000

dead
tree

TURRET 40B

900

800

MILECASTLE 41

Camp Site

Bogle
Hole

VALLUM

Winshields Farm

B 6318

4½ GREENHEAD

of consolidated Wall, down to Thorny Doors before descending gently to Cawfield Quarry Picnic Site overlooking the quarry pond. Leave the car park, go along the road and take the next right over the bridge crossing Haltwhistle Burn. Immediately after the bridge take a wall stile on the left to pass to the left of Burnhead Cottage and follow the gentle rise to a ladder stile next to a six-bar gate.

Across the next field is the farm at Great Chesters and upon reaching it can be seen the outlines, some exposed, of Aesica Roman Fort. Head for the trees on Cockmount Hill and take a ladder stile into the pine wood. Follow a winding, narrow, stony path through the trees and exit the wood via a ladder stile with the now grassy track leading to rising ground. Here the path starts the traverse of the Nine Nicks of Thirlwall to the left of the residual Wall now reduced to a grassy, rubble ridge topped occasionally with a field wall. After an initial climb the path soon descends to a dramatically situated turret overlooking Walltown Gap. In the Gap, flagstones assist over

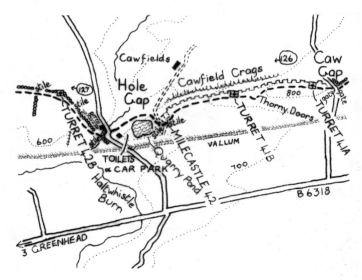

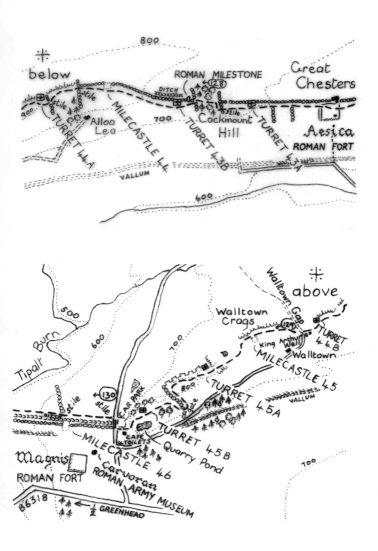

below

800

+

ROMAN MILESTONE

Great Chesters

DITCH

128

900

stile stile

TURRET 44A

Alloo Lea

MILECASTLE 44

700

Cockmount Hill

stile

TURRET 43B

TURRET 43A

Aesica
ROMAN FORT

VALLUM

600

above

500

Walltown Gap

+

Walltown Crags

129

TURRET 44B

Tipalt Burn

600

700

King Arthur's Well

MILECASTLE 45

Walltown

130

800

TURRET 45A

VALLUM

sluice

stile

CAR PARK

stile

TURRET 45B

CAFÉ & TOILETS

Quarry Pond

700

MILECASTLE 46

Magnis
ROMAN FORT

Carvoran
ROMAN ARMY MUSEUM

B6318

½ GREENHEAD

the damp ground resulting from the spring water from King Arthur's Well. Climb to the ridge and stay on the high ground to pass an old quarry and Walltown Crags before the course of the Wall is rudely interrupted by Walltown Quarry. Descend by the field wall to a kissing gate on to a path through trees and into the quarry. Leave the quarry, with its refreshment facilities, and turn right on to the road heading north. Almost immediately on the left is the sudden re-emergence of the Ditch. Take the signpost (FP Thirlwall Castle ¾m) on the left and follow the Ditch to a ladder stile with a view of the hamlet of Longbyre. Descend to the trees through which can be seen the inner ruins of Thirlwall Castle and drop down to the bridge at Holmhead House. On reaching Thirlwall Castle follow the waymarks through a gate and down the track with Tipalt Burn on the left. Do not cross the railway track but take the gate on the left where a path, between the river and the railway, leads straight into Greenhead.

DAY ELEVEN

Greenhead to Alston

Distance	17 miles
Highest Point	1,112 feet
Height Ascended	2,451 feet
Going	Moderate
Map	O.S. Explorer OL31 & OL43

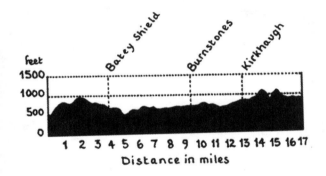

The route now heads southwards and, for the most part, is in the valley of the South Tyne. Eleven years after the Pennine Way was opened in 1965 the railway line from Alston to Haltwhistle was closed. In 2004, using part of the disused track, the 23-mile South Tyne Trail was opened from the river's source to Hexham. Today's route is a combination of this trail and the Pennine Way but will also touch upon and be near to a much more ancient route – the Maiden Way. This is a Roman road from Kirkby Thore, near Appleby, to Carvoran Fort on Hadrian's Wall, and from it AW got his 'last glimpse . . . of the ridge from Thirlwall to Housesteads'. Soon after leaving Greenhead the path links up with the southern section of Mark Richards' *The Roman Ring* (see Day 9).

Thirlwall Castle

The South Tyne Valley did not escape the attention of the mining prospectors and during the nineteenth century produced large quantities of coal as well as lead and other ores. The path passes the ruins of one of the area's major collieries, Lambley, before arriving at Lambley Viaduct with its soaring arches that span the South Tyne. Completed in 1852, and now a Grade II listed building, it has been in the care of the North Pennines Heritage Trust since 1996.

The disused railway is followed for 4 miles to Slaggyford where the Pennine Way is rejoined for the rest of the day's journey to Alston. The Roman theme continues as the path goes round the Roman fort of Whitley Castle. The stage ends at the Jacob Walton Memorial — a recently restored (2004) local tribute to a highly respected mine owner — built after a public subscription list was instigated by his workers.

Lambley Viaduct

Route Description

From the Greenhead Hotel go uphill and just before the no through road sign take a track (FP Blenkinsopp Common ¾m) on the left that swings right at the bottom of the slope to pass through a gate by a cottage garage. Take the wet track keeping the fence/hedge on the right and continue forward along the edge of the field to the corner of a plantation on the right. Here, cross a stile, take the steps down to a track and go right to

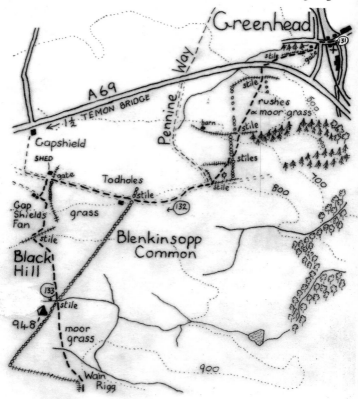

the verge of the busy A69. Cross this with care aiming for wooden steps just to the right, leading up to a stile at the top of the embankment. At the stile there are two footpath signs — take the one leading half right to meet a row of hawthorns at the end of which is a ladder stile. The path ascends from this to another ladder stile in a wall. Cross and go immediately left over another stile, then bear right over a field of marsh grass aiming to the right of a solitary wind-blown tree. At a stile leading on to a track, yet again, the Pennine Way is joined with the luxury of intermittent waymarks. Take the grassy path opposite, to a ladder stile in a wall, to arrive at a gate just before a ruined stone building. Go straight ahead across the meadow to a gate with a Pennine Way sign. Bear left, crossing stone slabs, to the ruins of derelict barns at Gap Shields Fan. Go left to the fence and, just before a gate, go right climbing to a stile in the fence. Here a faint track meanders in a generally southerly direction to a ladder stile to the left of the O.S. column on the top of Black Hill. The path goes over marsh grass to a fence corner.

Continue with the fence on the right dropping gently to bend left to cross a boardwalk and a ladder stile. Stay with the fence on the right and cross a footbridge to arrive at a waymarker post beside the fence. Go left here over marsh grass in a generally easterly direction towards the buildings of Highside keeping to the high ground. Two prominent gates to the right of the farm come into view. Here drop right towards Greenriggs farm, which can be seen below, to a stile in the fence. Descend the field to the farm and take the paving stones to a ladder stile. Go right, around the farm buildings to the access track and follow it to the minor road. A finger posted footbridge over Kellah Burn leads to Batey Shield where waymarks point the way through the buildings. The path leads to a footbridge over Hartley Burn. *About half way between Batey Shield and the Hartley Burn footbridge a path comes in from the left and it is at this point that the main route is joined by the recommended alternative 'off season' route — see Day 9 for further details.* Turn sharp left and head for the high ground where a path will be found which ascends the rise to the ruins of High House.

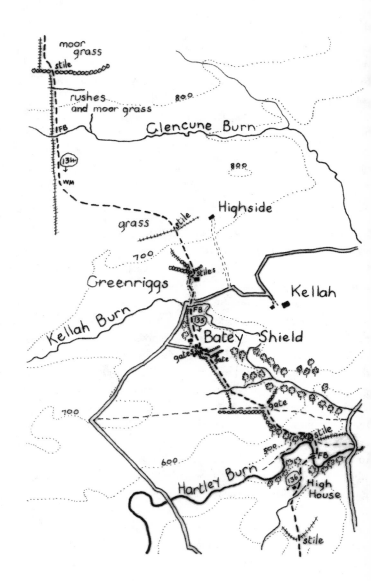

moor
grass

stile

rushes
and moor grass

800

FB

Glencune Burn

134

800

WM

grass

stile

Highside

700

Greenriggs

stiles

Kellah

Kellah Burn

FB
135

Batey Shield

gate

gate

700

gate

stile

FB

600

500

136

High
House

Hartley Burn

stile

The path follows more boggy ground, with at one point extensive use of slabs, to pass the remains of Lambley Colliery to a stile on to the A689. Here the Pennine Way is left for a short while for two purposes. Firstly to take in the magnificent Lambley Viaduct as it crosses high above the River South Tyne and secondly to escape a boggy stretch of the Pennine Way for a spell of easy walking on the South Tyne Trail. Go left, then turn left at a road (SP Featherstone 4m) and after a few yards go right on a footpath (FP Lambley ⅓m). This goes up a cottage drive, over a stile and into a meadow. Continue straight ahead to a stile, then a kissing gate and bear right over the next meadow to a gate in the fence. Take the underpass to another gate and go right, past the cottages on to a minor road. Turn right, through the hamlet of Lambley, passing the little church of St Mary and St. Patrick. Just before the A689, take a path on the left (FP Lambley Viaduct ¼m; Coanwood 1m) through a kissing gate and follow the lane. Another gate leads onto an overgrown metalled path which heads downhill to a wicket gate at the edge of woodland. Descend the steps to a junction of paths and go forward (FP South Tyne Trail South; Slaggyford 3¾m) to swing right beside the pillar of the viaduct then left to cross a footbridge. The path climbs a steep flight of steps and then crosses boardwalks to pass beside the old Lambley Railway Station up to the right. Climb to the old trackbed and go left, passing over a minor road.

The path stays with the trackbed to a point where large boulders obstruct the way at Burnstones and continues on to Slaggyford. The tree-lined route is highly attractive and there are frequent and unexpected views left into the valley of the South Tyne and the hills beyond.

Slaggyford announces itself with the station platform on the right and the former station master's house (complete with station sign) opposite. Go left down the road to reach the A689 and turn right to where a minor road (SP Barhaugh Hall) leaves on the left. Almost immediately pick up a delightful riverside path which passes underneath the striking viaduct at Lintley, goes left over a footbridge and rises to a farm track. Cross the

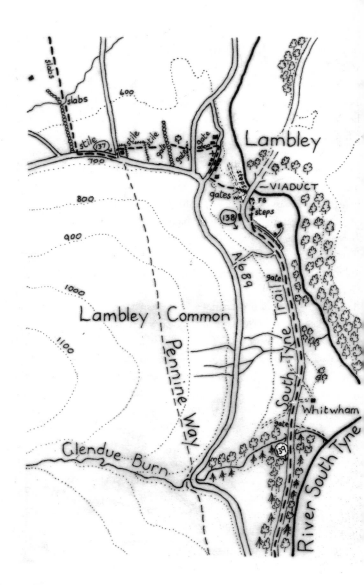

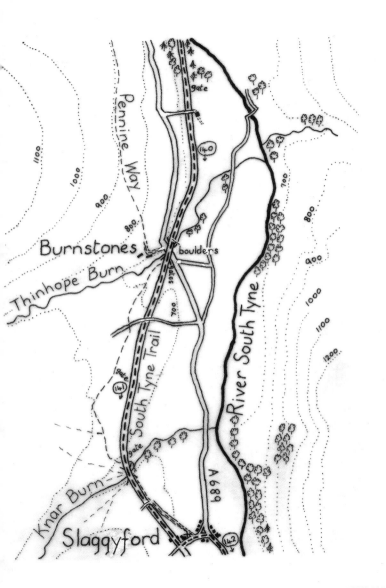

Pennine Way

River South Tyne

gate

140

700

800

900

1100

1000

900

800

Burnstones

boulders

Thinhope Burn

700

South Tyne Trail

1000

1100

1200

gate
141

gate

Knar Burn

A 689

Slaggyford

142

track and, with the railway embankment on the left, go over undulating ground and many stiles to arrive at Kirkhaugh. Turn left down towards the railway track and just before the bridge go right onto a farm track and head south away from the railway track (this section is no longer disused and carries the South Tynedale Railway) to rejoin the A689 by a telephone box.

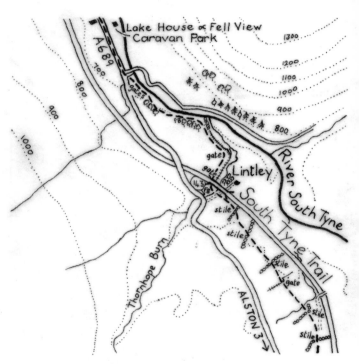

Cross the road, go through a narrow gap in the low wall and rise on a good path through trees. After a kissing gate look for a stile towards the right hand field corner onto a track which becomes a grassy path curving around the earthwork embankments. These mark the site of

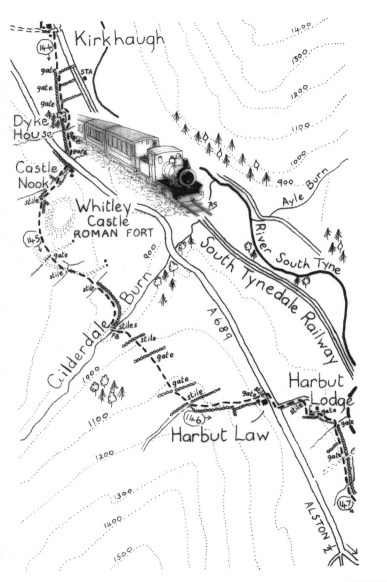

Kirkhaugh

144

STA

gate
gate
gate

Dyke
House

gate
gate

Castle
Nook

stile

Whitley
Castle
ROMAN FORT

145

gate

stile

Cilderdale Burn

900

stiles

FB

stile

gate

1000

gate

stile

1100

Harbut
Law

146

1200

1300

1400

1500

Ayle Burn

River South Tyne

South Tynedale Railway

A 689

RS

Harbut
Lodge

gate

stile

gate

gate

gate

147

ALSTON 2

900

1000

1100

1200

1300

1400

The Market Cross

Alston

Whitley Castle, a Roman fort and signal station. The bridge over the lovely Gilderdale Burn is reached which is left on a good grass path climbing through a succession of gates to the top of the rise. Where a gate leads onto a wide walled track, take the wall stile to the left of it and bear left over marsh grass to reach the buildings of Harbut Law where the A689 is rejoined. Turn right for a few yards to the access road to Harbut Lodge and leave it at a wall stile on the right. The signed path crosses meadows towards the river, stays close to it and after passing a dilapidated seat (mentioned by AW in his *Pennine Way Companion*) soon meets the A689. Turn left to the junction with the A686, with Alston's War Memorial opposite, and cross the fine South Tyne Bridge to finish this stage at the Town Hall and the Jacob Walton Memorial.

DAY TWELVE

Alston to Milburn

Distance	16¾ miles
Highest Point	2,575 feet
Height Ascended	2,500 feet
Going	Moderate with one steep climb
Map	O.S. Explorer OL31

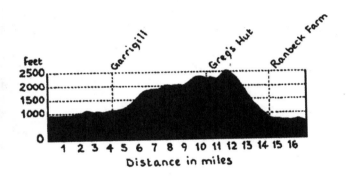

Alston is situated within the North Pennines Area of Outstanding Natural Beauty and its claim to fame is that it is reputed to be 'the highest market town in England'. However, like other settlements along the journey, it was also a centre for the lead mining industry. With its cobbled streets, seventeeth-century stone houses and the Market Cross donated by a former townsman who became Lord Mayor of London, it is easy to see why it was used as a setting for the films of *Jane Eyre* and *Oliver Twist*. Charles Dickens visited Alston in 1838 whilst working on his novel *Nicholas Nickleby*.

Appropriately, as this is the Pennine Journey, today's stage returns to the Pennines and it is one of the most strenuous of the journey, particularly if the opportunity is taken to divert to the summit

Bridge over the River South Tyne, Alston

of Cross Fell. From there on a clear day there are distant views of the Lake District fells and, across the Solway Firth, the Southern Uplands of Scotland. Cross Fell, 'the monarch of the Pennines', is the highest point in England outside AW's beloved Lakeland. It was his intention to cross into the Eden Valley via Cross Fell and had he done so his route would have mirrored most of today's stage, but bad weather brought an enforced change of plan. Our route, though, will again be following the Pennine Way along the valley of the South Tyne to Garrigill before striking over the shoulder of Cross Fell.

This part of the journey takes advantage of an old corpse road used by the people of Garrigill to take their dead for burial in St Laurence's Church, Kirkland, until their own church was built in the nineteenth century. As it drops into Kirkland another historical site is visible – the Hanging Walls of Mark Anthony. No, these are

Greg's Hut

not more evidence of Roman occupation but are the remains of strip lynchets that were cultivated 1,500 years before the Romans came to Britain. From Kirkland the route goes across fields and Crowdundle Beck (which may, or may not, have a bridge to facilitate a dry crossing) to arrive at Milburn with its huge village green and maypole.

Route Description

From the Jacob Walton Memorial return to the bridge over the River South Tyne and just before the bridge, take a footpath on the left (PW sign).

The path follows the river, breaks out of the woodland and continues through several fields with clear stiles and Pennine Way route markers. Go through the farmyard at Bleagate and, after passing Low Sillyhall, rejoin the river. Cross the river at a footbridge and continue upstream on a delightful path on the south bank.

The Market Cross

Alston

When the path meets a road turn left and follow it into Garrigill. Pass the George and Dragon pub and post office in the centre of the village and at the 'no through road' sign turn right passing the Primitive Methodist Chapel (1885). Follow the walled track uphill past the new Open Access signs and continue over Black Band with shake holes in the surrounding area.

The track heads south and, after going through the second gate, continues across open moorland, passing Pikeman Hill and Long Man Hill. Ignore two paths which join the main track from the left and right and continue climbing towards the old mine workings at Black Gut visible on the skyline. The track becomes rocky and near the top of the workings a cairn marks a path junction. Take the right fork along Blackstone Edge – straight on being a direct route to Cross Fell.

River South Tyne

ALSTON

Nattrass Gill

Low Nest

High Nest

wooded hollow
old quarry

Low Cowgap

Black Burn

Bleagate

Low Sillyhall

GARRIGILL 1½

gate
stile
stile

stile
stile

149

stile
FB
stiles

stile

gate
stile

stile

stile

gate
stile

150

stile

gate
stile

FB

stile

stile

1000

1100

1000

1100

1200

1300

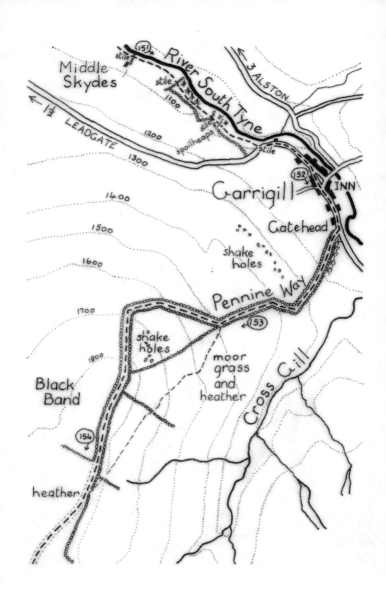

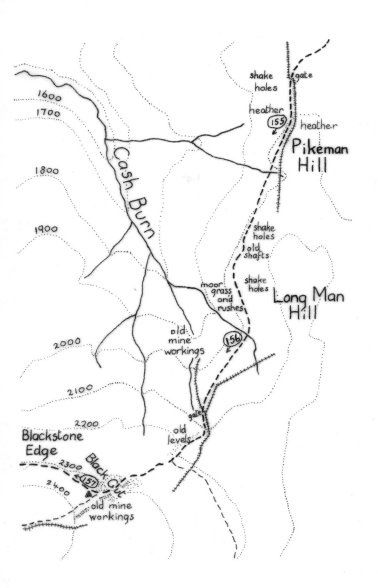

shake
holes

gate

heather

155

heather

Pikeman
Hill

1600

1700

1800

1900

Cash Burn

shake
holes

old
shafts

moor
grass
and
rushes

shake
holes

Long Man
Hill

old
mine
workings

156

2000

2100

gate

2200

old
levels

Blackstone
Edge

Black Cut

2300

157

2400

old mine
workings

Greg's Hut, a former mine cottage and now a bothy, is soon reached and is an ideal place to stop for lunch, offering shelter if the weather is not too good and great views to the north if it is fine. Soon the highest point of the day is reached at an engraved boulder, which marks the point where the route leaves the Pennine Way. *To include a visit to the summit of Cross Fell (at 2930 feet the highest point on the Pennine Way), follow the PW arrow on the boulder for an out and back 1-mile round trip with 350 feet of ascent. The path is indistinct at first and crosses some boggy ground but it is just a matter of heading uphill aiming for the large cairns.*

The main route follows the Kirkland arrow straight ahead, crosses over the watershed and then starts a long descent to Kirkland. The track is indistinct at times but after joining an old mining track improves in quality lower down, with good views across the Vale of Eden to the Lakeland fells.

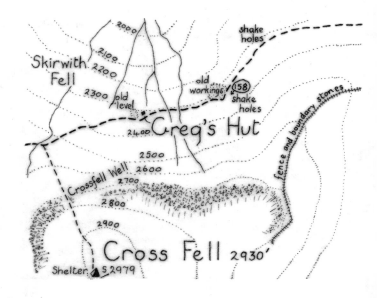

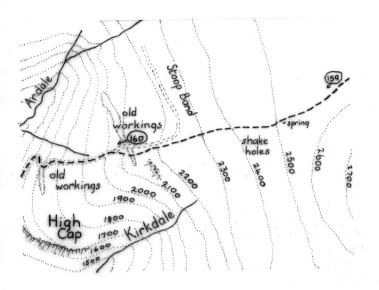

The route does not enter Kirkland but just before the first buildings (with a parking space opposite) turns left on to a bridleway (SP Ranbeck). The path passes through farmland and is not obvious on the ground. Head south-east, through a gate at a field corner and keep to the left edge of the large field. Exit the field through the third gate into a small field with the farm at Ranbeck ahead. Do not go through the farmyard but loop left around the buildings to join the metalled road. Turn left along the road, past the ancient cultivation terraces of the Hanging Walls of Mark Anthony, to the farm buildings at Wythwaite. The bridleway heads south through another gated field to enter some woodland. Pass over a footbridge made of two old railway sleepers. Crowdundle Beck is presently without a bridge (the latest one was washed away in recent floods but there are plans to replace it) or stepping stones and must be forded — with or without boots! *If the beck is in spate then return to Wythwaite and take the farm track to Blencarn from where a minor road leads to Milburn.*

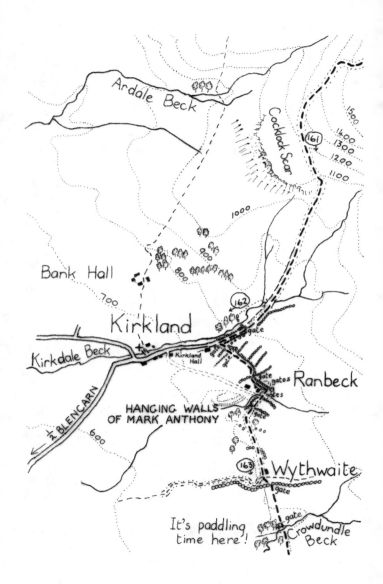

Ardale Beck

Cocklock Scar

161

1500
1400
1300
1200
1100

1000

Bank Hall

900
800

700

162

Kirkland

gate

Kirkdale Beck

Kirkland Hall

gate gates
gates
gates
Ranbeck

BLENCARN

HANGING WALLS
OF MARK ANTHONY

600

gate

163

Wythwaite

gate

It's paddling
time here!

gate

Crowdundle Beck

Head up the embankment, turning right at the top to parallel the beck for approximately 200 yards until a huge oak tree is reached. Here follow a faint path left, through bracken and tall grass, past some isolated trees with the furthest one bearing a waymarker arrow. Head for the wall junction and cross into the farmland through the gate in the wall (ignoring the stile in the fence). The route continues over stiles with waymarker discs through a number of fields to join a track leading to the village of Milburn with its expansive village green and magnificent maypole.

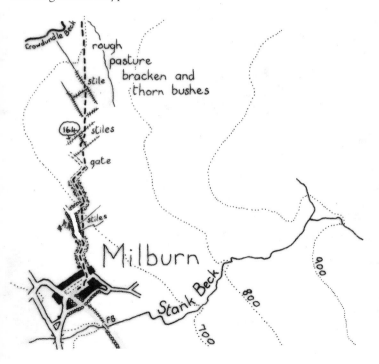

DAY THIRTEEN

Milburn to Appleby

Distance	8¼ miles
Highest Point	719 feet
Height Ascended	771 feet
Going	Easy but slow going
Map	O.S. Explorer OL19

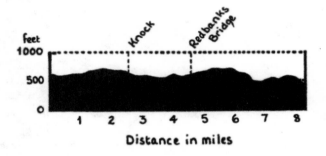

This is the day when the path makes its way across the broad wide plain of the River Eden, a 'confusion of flat meadows and wide pastures', from the foothills of the Pennines to Appleby.

Milburn, nestling below Great Dun Fell, is a splendid example of a medieval fortified village. The houses are situated on the four sides of the rectangular 4½-acre village green, which is dominated by a huge maypole said to be on the site of a Celtic burial ground. With only one road into the village from the south, entrances at each corner (closed off each winter) and narrow passages between each house, the settlement was easily defended from raiders – the green acting as a huge sheep pen. Some of the houses still have no windows facing away from the green as the consequent lack of light would have kept the village hidden from passing reivers. On the outskirts of the village are St Cuthbert's Church,

Milburn Green and Maypole

with its Norman nave and chancel, and Howgill Castle. Never a castle in the accepted sense, it comprises two pele towers and dates from the fourteenth century but was extensively renovated in the mid-twentieth century.

Milburn has one other distinction in Britain – its helm wind. This is a local wind caused by a specific geographical feature, in this case Cross Fell, and strong winds can last for days in the area of Brough to Brampton with Milburn at its epicentre. It is possible that AW was on the receiving end of this as he experienced atrocious weather on his travels between Alston and Kirkby Stephen. AW passed through Milburn 'with two churches and an inn' on his journey by road through Appleby to Soulby, but our path is much more scenic as it stays close to the Pennines. It passes through Knock, a small farming community dominated by Knock Pike; a lovely tranquil place with its one street lined by attractive cottages.

At Dufton (a farmstead where doves are reared) the path briefly rejoins the Pennine Way. The village, overlooked by Dufton Pike, has a large green as its centrepiece and a prominent water fountain given by

Dufton

the London Lead Company. From here it is a tranquil 3 miles through meadow and woodland to Appleby.

Route Description

Across the village green opposite the far set of football posts take a path (FP Knock) through a field, crossing a footbridge over Stank Beck (very boggy), and then a stile. Follow the path across the fields, keeping the fence on the right, and go around the left hand side of the farm building of Low Howgill farm. Go over a stile to reach a concrete track, turn right and cross over a cattle grid then a small bridge. Immediately take a rough track on the left uphill and after the track levels bear right at a fork to pass High Slakes Farm. At a gate follow the waymark half left across the field to a stile in the facing wall. Keep to the left hand side of the field and at the end of the trees head for a gate in the wall ahead. Once through the gate turn sharp left and head for a gap stile. Cross the village playground at Milburn Grange and take another gap stile in the wall corner. Turn right between the buildings and locate a track on the left between a farmhouse and a row of garages through a gate (FP Knock).

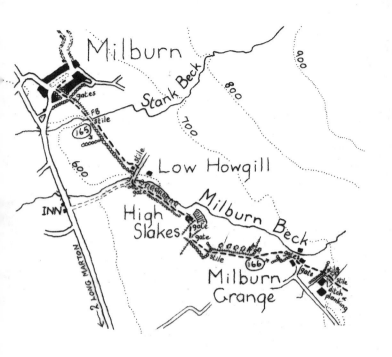

Follow the path across the fields and join a track leading to Close House. Go through the farmyard and onto the drive to meet a lane. Turn right to pass Close House Cottage and then take the right hand gate on the left (SP Knock). Go directly across the fields towards farm buildings and join a track which goes around the buildings to meet the road at Knock. Turn left and, once through the village, take a signposted wall stile on the left shortly after a bench seat dedicated to Jimmy Allan. Head down the field and at the bottom bear left to reach a footbridge in the corner. Turn right, cross a wall stile and head for a gate into the churchyard. The twelfth-century St Cuthbert's church is well worth a visit. Take a narrow wall stile to the left of the

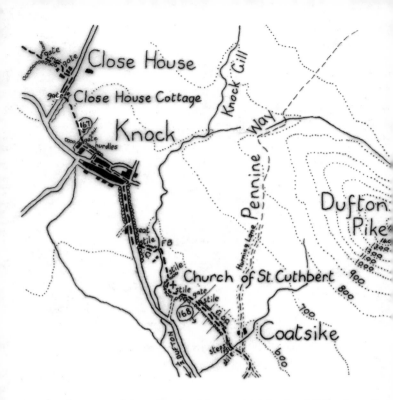

church gates and, ignoring the drive, go straight ahead following a line of mature trees with a fence and then a wall on the right. At a gate, go through a field to another gate and then on to an overgrown track between trees and hedgerows.

Soon go down steps, cross a footbridge, then another stile and follow the path until it meets a wide track. This is again the Pennine Way which is joined for a short distance but soon left when the track bends right to reach a surfaced road. Go left into Dufton but before the village green, at a fork, take the right hand road and, keeping the old school on the left, locate a path at the end of a row of terraced cottages (FP Wood Lane to Brampton). Follow the track, descending

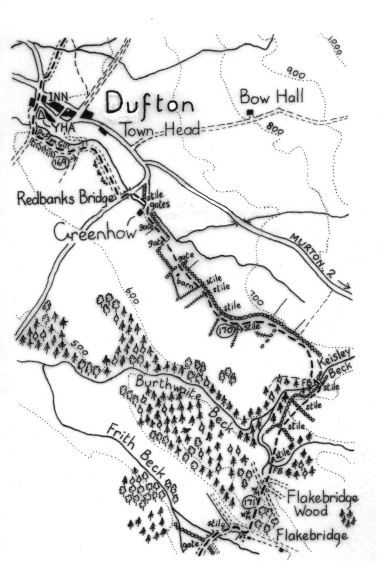

INN

△ YHA

169

Dufton

Town Head

Bow Hall

900

800

1000

Redbanks Bridge

Greenhow

stile
gates

gate

gate

gate

barn

stile

stile

stile

170

stile

600

500

700

MURTON 2

Keisley

Beck

FB

stile

stile

stile

Burthwaite Beck

stile

FB

Frith Beck

171

Flakebridge Wood

Flakebridge

stile

gate

through trees, to cross a footbridge over Dufton Gill. Ascend the stoned path ahead and at the next junction of paths go left. Where the path meets a wider track, go left again and then right on a path (FP Redbanks Bridge). Cross a footbridge and turn left, following the gill upstream through Dufton Ghyll Wood to eventually reach the road at Redbanks Bridge. Turn left, cross the bridge, and immediately go right on a path (FP Keisley and Flakebridge). Follow the beck over a wooden footbridge to a wall stile and join a concrete track. Go through two metal gates passing to the left of all the buildings and continue on through three fields. After a large stone barn in the third field go uphill slightly to a stile in the field corner by a metal gate and cross a further four fields, keeping the wall on the left. Approaching trees at the far end of the fourth field the path bears right to a footbridge. Cross the bridge over Keisley Beck, turn left then immediately right over a wall stile and go uphill keeping the wall and tree plantation on the right to a stile, which will soon be seen directly ahead. Cross the next field, with the plantation still to the right, to a wall stile in the corner and bear left over the next field and downhill to a ladder stile. Over the wall bear right and follow the path across a small footbridge and on through the wood to join a track. Go right and at the next junction of paths go straight ahead following a public footpath. The faint path goes on through the trees and soon descends to reach a track at the edge of the wood. The buildings of Black Bill can be seen to the left. Turn right to a junction of paths and go straight ahead to a stile by a gate leading into a meadow (FP Hungriggs Lane).

Go through the field and over a small stone bridge, then ahead through a second field. Pass through a gate and proceed with woods on the left to meet a grassy farm track. Here, turn right to a stile in the wall and head uphill to a further stile in a fence by a gate. Go uphill across the field to another stile by a huge ash tree and continue with a hedge on the right to reach the farm at Hungriggs. Go through the gate between the farm buildings to join a track which leads uphill to meet a lane. Turn left and follow the lane to a T-junction. Turn left and follow the road under the A66 and then immediately right past the school and railway station. *Railway enthusiasts may wish to take the opportunity afforded by a signed pedestrian footpath to visit Appleby station on the Settle – Carlisle line. Cross the tracks over the footbridge where signs point to the town centre.* At the next main road junction turn left and then cross the River Eden by the bridge to reach the centre of Appleby with its market square, St Lawrence's Church and the adjacent Low Cross.

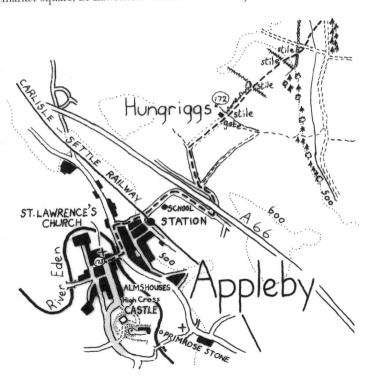

DAY FOURTEEN

Appleby to Kirkby Stephen

Distance	16 miles
Highest Point	673 feet
Height Ascended	1,585 feet
Going	Easy
Map	O.S. Explorer OL19

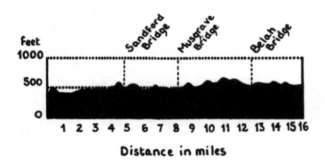

Appleby plays a very important part in the story of this Pennine Journey. It was here that AW decided to abandon his journey, dispirited by the appalling weather that had delayed him and disrupted his plans. However, fortunately for us, he had a change of heart and at three o'clock (and with 'nearly sixty miles to travel' and only the remainder of that day and two more days left) he set off for Kirkby Stephen.

Appleby, or Appleby-in-Westmorland as it is now known, occupies a strategic position in the Eden Valley, and is an historic town with origins going back over 1,000 years. For the early part of that period it was actually in Scotland and during the period when the border fluctuated, its Norman castle dating from the twelfth century was seized by the Scots when they invaded the area in 1174. For much of the following 500 years it was in the ownership of the Clifford family and Lady Anne Clifford restored the castle in the mid-seventeenth century, making it one of her principal residences. She died in Appleby in 1676 at the great age of eighty-six and was buried, alongside her mother, in St Lawrence's church.

Low Cross, Appleby

The picturesque, wide main street, Boroughgate, links the castle and the church, and has a cross at each end — a seventeenth-century High Cross near the castle and an eighteenth-century copy, the Low Cross, by the church. Also on Boroughgate are twelve almshouses and a chapel built by Lady Anne and now known as the Hospital of St Anne. The Appleby Horse Fair, established by charter in 1685 for horse trading, is world famous and each June attracts large numbers of travelling folk. However, a more modern link to this journey is that the town is on the Settle to Carlisle railway.

The route is almost entirely within the Eden Valley and passes through a succession of charming villages which includes Great

Brough Castle

Ormside with its Viking origins. Here, in the early nineteenth century, the Ormside Bowl was found – a particularly fine example of Saxon metalwork from the ninth century, which is now in York Museum. The path departs briefly from the Eden Valley to pass the ruins of Brough Castle – another Norman castle once owned by the Clifford family and, again, restored by Lady Anne.

From Church Brough the path heads south and, after a delightful short stretch along the banks of the River Belah, one of Eden's tributaries, passes through Winton to reach Kirkby Stephen. Here there could well be opportunities to compare notes with other long distance footpath walkers, as this is a recognised 'end of stage' along AW's Coast to Coast Walk. In his guide he describes it as 'a place for licking wounds and replenishing supplies'.

Route Description

From St Lawrence's church by the Low Cross walk up Boroughgate on the left hand side and take a few minutes to admire the almshouses and chapel, founded by Lady Anne Clifford. Continue to the High Cross, bear right at the castle gates (Shaws Wiend) and follow the wall enclosing the castle grounds. When the road turns away to the right stay with the wall and descend Castle Bank to the River Eden.

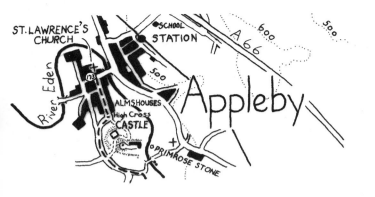

The route takes a kissing gate on the right before the footbridge (FP Ormside) but a very short diversion over the footbridge leads, immediately on the left, to the 'Primrose Stone' – one of ten Eden Benchmark sculptures commissioned by the East Cumbria Countryside Project and local communities along the Eden. Tomorrow's route passes another one. After a period of confinement the path emerges in a large field alongside the river. Follow the river, crossing a series of stiles and passing through a copse to reach a larger wood next to the river. Enter the wood over a stile and follow the path by the river, soon crossing a footbridge over a beck and continue on the riverside path which eventually leaves the Eden up a flight of wooden steps. Stay on top of the bank following the edge of the wood. The path now slopes down to a footbridge in the wooded confines of Jeremy Gill and then rises alongside a small feeder. Emerging at the top, follow the hedgerow to the left to reach a stile by a gate and then turn left on a broad green path. Over to the left is a glimpse of the Ormside Viaduct carrying the Settle to Carlisle line. On reaching a farm track, take the railway underpass and stay with the enclosed track until it bends sharp left. Go through the right hand gate, cross a field passing a small pond and take two stiles to reach the road at Great Ormside.

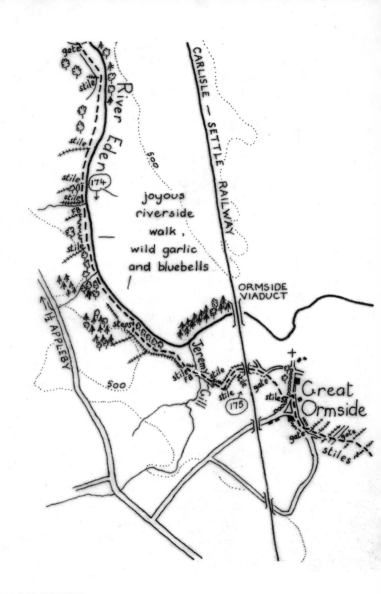

gate

stile

River Eden

stile

stile
stile

174

stile

CARLISLE — SETTLE RAILWAY

joyous
riverside
walk,
wild garlic
and bluebells

ORMSIDE
VIADUCT

1½ APPLEBY

steps

500

Jeremy Gill

stile

stile

stile

175

gate

stile

stiles

Great
Ormside

gate

gate

stiles

500

Turn left and immediately right and soon, after passing a farmhouse (1687), take a footpath on the left and follow waymarks across fields via stiles and gates to reach a narrow lane. Turn right through Little Ormside and after passing a magnificent cedar tree at Terrys Farm, the track continues straight ahead (BW Blacksyke and Warcop) to Tricklebanks Wood. Follow the edge of the wood eventually entering it through a wooden gate in the field corner, to emerge at Blacksyke Farm. Follow the farm track to reach Sandford Bridge but do not cross. Take a path on the right (FP Birks Head and Warcop) and turn left at the next stile to cross the bungalow drive. Go through a wooden gate straight ahead, uphill along the field edge to another wooden gate.

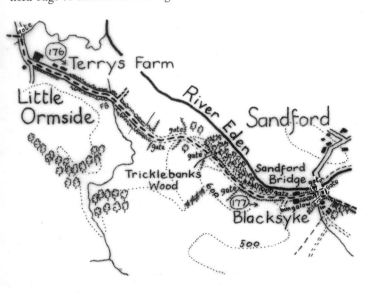

Continue by the hedge to a metal gate and then on to reach an enclosed farm track. Take this track and on meeting another track, turn left down to a concrete road then turn right. This road leads to a small lane and here turn left to Warcop Old Bridge. Do not cross but go through a gap stile (FP Ploughlands) and follow the path along the river to a metal gate.

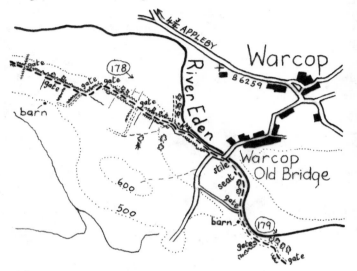

Here the path gently rises along a wide green track before turning away from the river to arrive at a stile overlooking Ploughlands Farm. Drop down the field to meet another stile in the wall corner. Turn left, keeping to the right of the fence, to reach a footbridge and stile onto a concrete road and turn right to reach the road at Little Musgrave. Turn left to a footpath (FP Musgrave Bridge) on the left, soon after a road junction. The path drops down across a rough patch of land then through fields along the river bank. When the field edge curves right away from the river, look out for a stile down the embankment to the left. The path passes the remains of the old railway bridge through thick undergrowth and trees by the river to reach Musgrave Bridge. Cross the bridge and take a path on the right (FP St Theobald's Church). This lovely little church, beautifully situated by the river, lies a little below the village. The path turns away from the river just before the church and climbs quite steeply to reach a small lane into Great Musgrave. Turn right and almost immediately right again (FP Hall Garth) to a gate on the left.

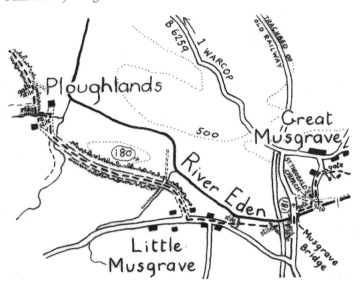

Cross to the right, past the cottages, to a stile in a short stretch of wall with Hall Garth Farm straight ahead. Drop down towards the farm to reach the lane at a gate. Turn right then immediately right again at a farm track to cross a bridge over Swindale Beck. Take a path on the left (BW Church Brough and Brough Sowerby) keeping close to the beck and at a fenced field corner head directly towards a metal gate. Head slightly right of the tree covered knoll to pass through a wooden gate then half right towards a stone barn passing through another wooden gate. Here a grass track gradually improves to become a stone track and on reaching another track follow this left into Church Brough.

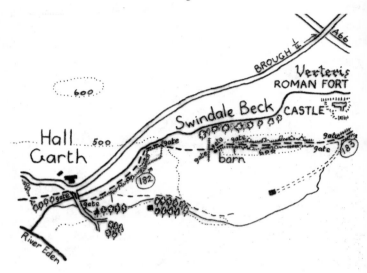

From the village green turn right along the lane and use an underpass on the left to cross to the far side of the busy A685. Turn right and use the grass verge by the A685 leaving it very soon by a stile on the left (FP Brough Sowerby). Ascend the field aiming for a clump of trees on the right beside which is a stile. Cross three fields, ignoring a stile on the right in the second of these, to reach Sowerby Park Farm. Go to the right of the farm through a gap stile in a wall corner onto a farm track, turn right and follow it to the lane at Brough Sowerby. Turn left and go past Hollins View Farm to reach a stony farm track on the right (BW Bloan). Follow the track until it turns away left and take the footpath, through the gate on the right, which drops down past a ruined barn to

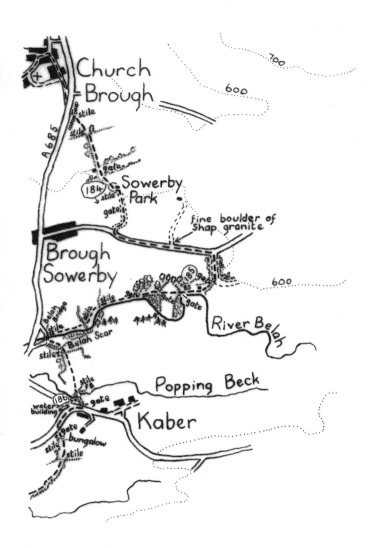

Church
Brough

A685

stile
stile

gate

(184)
stile

gate

Sowerby
Park

fine boulder of
Shap granite

Brough
Sowerby

(185)

600

stile

stile

Belah
Bridge

River Belah

stile

Belah Scar

stiles

stile
FB

(18b)

gate

Popping Beck

water
building

Kaber

gate
bungalow

stile
stile

the River Belah, a tributary of the Eden. Where the river loops away to the left, go through a metal gate on the right and cross the field, to rejoin the river. Stay with the river, passing Belah Scar on the far bank, to reach Belah Bridge and turn left over the bridge to take the path on the left (FP Kaber). Climb the bank on the right to a stile over a wire fence at the top and cross the field to another stile. Keep straight ahead and where the fence bends away to the right continue straight on to a stile by a gate. Cross Popping Beck by a bridge to reach the lane out of Kaber and turn right. Take a green track just before a bungalow on the left, to a stile by a gate. From here the path is to the left of the hedge but moves to the right over the next stile.

Just before reaching the bottom of a long field take a wooden footbridge and gate into the next field and almost immediately go over the stile on the right. Head to a stile and gate, with the roofs of Winton visible, to reach the lane at Winton and turn right into the village. Follow the main street with the village green on the left and the impressive Winton Manor House on the right. Where the road bends right to join the A685 go straight ahead and take a footpath on the left (FP Eden Place). The path, enclosed at first, leads to a small field and then continues straight ahead to the right of the fence. Cross the footbridge over Mill Beck and upon emerging from the trees go half right to a stile in the wall corner. Go half left in the next field to a stile beneath a large sycamore tree. Cross four more fields by stiles to arrive at a lane. Turn right to pass Eden Place and reach the busy A685, turning left along it. Just before the bridge over the River Eden take a path (FP Low Mill Bridge) down steps to the left which crosses a footbridge over a small feeder then follows the river to the road at Lowmill Bridge. Join the road and keep straight ahead to a path (FP Hartley and Nateby) that crosses Hartley Beck over a footbridge and rejoins the bank of the River Eden. Follow the river past the cricket ground to reach Frank's Bridge. Over the bridge take the stone steps on the right and at the top a right turn will lead you to the Market Square in Kirkby Stephen town centre.

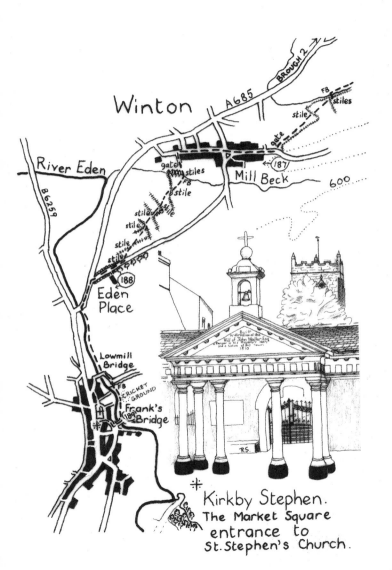

Winton

River Eden

B6259

A685

BROUGH 2

FB
stile   stiles

stile

gate   stile
gate stiles   187

Mill Beck

FB

stile

600

stile

stile

stile

stile

stile

188

Eden
Place

Lowmill
Bridge

FB

CRICKET
GROUND

Frank's
Bridge

189

Built
by direction of the
Will of John Waller Esq
a Banker in his Majesty's Navy
and a Native of this Town
1810

R.S.

✠ Kirkby Stephen.
The Market Square
entrance to
St. Stephen's Church.

DAY FIFTEEN

Kirkby Stephen to Garsdale Head

Distance	12¼ miles
Highest Point	1,483 feet
Height Ascended	1,909 feet
Going	Moderate with one steep climb
Map	O.S. Explorer OL19

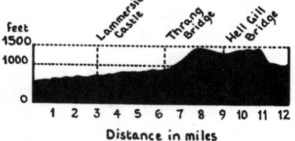

Today, from Kirkby Stephen down the Eden Valley and beyond to Garsdale Head, is one of the most delightful stages of this journey. For most of the day the route stays close to the River Eden, going through part of the valley known as Mallerstang, before finally passing close to the river's source.

Kirkby Stephen was AW's objective when he resumed his travels at Appleby. He had 'misgivings as to the wisdom of continuing the long walk' there when further awful weather meant that he only got as far as Soulby. Kirkby Stephen rivals Appleby as the premier market town of the Eden Valley and is an excellent centre for exploring the charms of the valley as well as the adjacent Yorkshire Dales and the nearby Howgill Fells. It was granted a market charter in 1361 by Edward

III and a further one in 1606 by James I to the Earl of Cumberland. The town's name is Saxon and derives from the twelfth-century St Stephen's 'kirk' within which is the ninth-century Loki Stone with its carving of a mythological Norse god. On the southern edge of the town are the pre-historic earthworks of Croglam Castle.

Frank's Bridge, Kirkby Stephen

Those of a literary nature should take time out at the start of the stage to enjoy a 'poetry path' – like the Eden Benchmarks, another East Cumbria Countryside Project. The path, which starts at Swingy Bridge over the Eden about ¾ mile from Frank's Bridge, consists of twelve short poems. These have been carved on blocks of stone situated at intervals on a circular path just over 1 mile long, with the added bonus of passing close to the Benchmark named 'Passage'. Today's walk, though, passes three of the poems.

The route accompanies the Eden passing Wharton Hall, a fine example of a fourteenth-century fortified manor house now a working farm, and the ruins of Lammerside Castle before arriving at the romantic ruins of Pendragon Castle. Its name derives from the legend that it was founded by Uther Pendragon, father of King Arthur, but there is no evidence that there was a building there until Norman times. Like Appleby and Brough castles it came into the possession of the Clifford family and was restored by Lady Anne in the mid-seventeenth century.

Appropriately the path soon takes The High Way – used by Lady Anne on her travels from Skipton to her estates in Westmorland – which was the main route from Hawes to Kirkby Stephen until the B6259 was opened as a turnpike road in the 1820s. As the path climbs just below Mallerstang Edge, across the valley is the striking Wild Boar Fell at 2,323 feet.

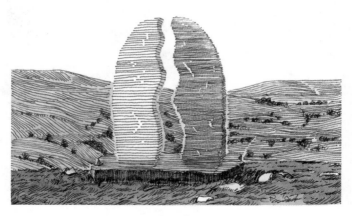

Water Cut

Soon 'Water Cut' – another Eden Benchmark – which has been prominent on the skyline during the ascent, is reached. The theme of this sculpture reflects the meanderings of the Eden below. After a high level terrace the path drops down to the Moorcock Inn, crossing over the infant River Ure.

Route Description

Leave the Market Square at the ornate south entrance to the Parish Church and return to Frank's Bridge. This is another junction of long distance footpaths: AW's Coast to Coast Walk; the 67-mile Eden Way from the river's source (close to today's route) to the sea near Carlisle; and the Lady Anne Clifford's Way. The Coast to Coast Walk, though, is left a mere 200 yards after turning right over Frank's Bridge where a path is taken on the right (FP Dod Gill). The other footpaths crisscross and accompany the route throughout the day. Follow the river, cross a small tributary by a footbridge and continue on a delightful, well defined path through meadows.

Ignore all side turnings, cross a disused railway, and a ford over Broad Ing Syke before reaching the B6259. Turn left towards Nateby and then

Kirkby Stephen.
The Market Square
entrance to
St. Stephen's Church.

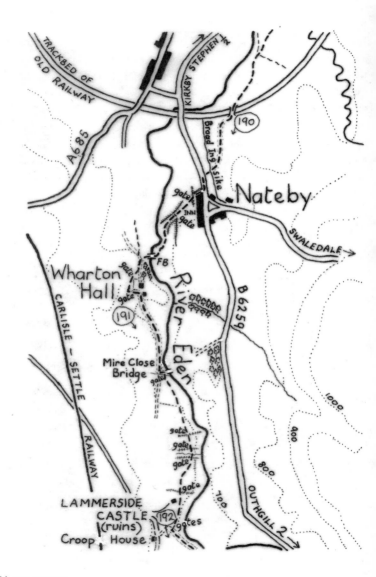

right (SP Public Bridleway) to pass through a gate and then over a stile to a small gate. Head diagonally left across the meadow to a footbridge over the river and on the other side walk up the meadow to a group of signs. The route crosses the farm road using a path (BW Bullgill or Mire Close Bridge) and passes through a gate to the right of the farm. At the next gate turn left, head down to Wharton Hall and turn right along a concrete track to arrive at Mire Close Bridge. Do not cross the bridge but continue on the concrete track for a few yards and leave it by a metalled gate on the left. From here the route heads diagonally left across a large meadow some distance from the river. On reaching a gate go straight ahead crossing two fields using the right hand pair of gates to arrive at the corner of a fenced, cultivated field. Lammerside Castle is diagonally right across the field and from the ruins drop down to a gate and signpost to join the track coming down from Croop House.

Turn left and go through a gate to follow the very clear track to the right of the river passing a lime kiln, in good condition, on the right. The path climbs to meet a metalled, unfenced road: turn left and drop down to a bridge over the River Eden. From the bridge the romantic ruins of Pendragon Castle are clearly visible and are well worth the short detour to make a closer inspection. Take a path just before the bridge (FP Shoregill) on the right and do not be put off by the 'Private Grounds' notice by a wooden barn as the path runs along the right hand field boundary. After a gill is bridged it goes across pasture land from where a glimpse of the castle can be seen across the river. The path continues over stiles, a plank bridge, a small wall, and a stone stile until a sign turns the path over a wooden stile to the left. Immediately pass through another stone stile on the right to Shoregill. Here, bear left downhill between the cottages and, immediately before the bridge over the Eden, turn right to follow a path through the wood which hugs the riverbank. Emerge from the wood and go slightly right to a stone stile which leads onto a track. Continue along this track, keeping right on entering the farmyard and return to the riverside path.

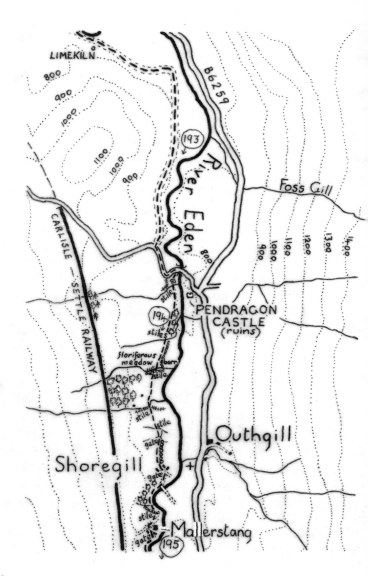

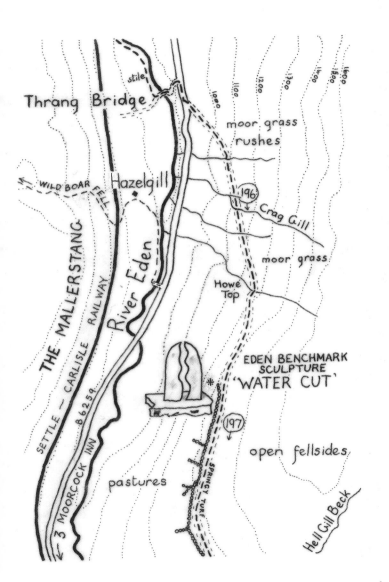

Thrang Bridge

stile

moor grass

rushes

WILD BOAR FELL

Hazelgill

196

Crag Gill

THE MALLERSTANG

River Eden

moor grass

Howe Top

EDEN BENCHMARK
SCULPTURE
'WATER CUT'

SETTLE — CARLISLE RAILWAY

B 6259

197

open fellsides

3 MOORCOCK INN

SPRINGY TURF

pastures

Hell Gill Beck

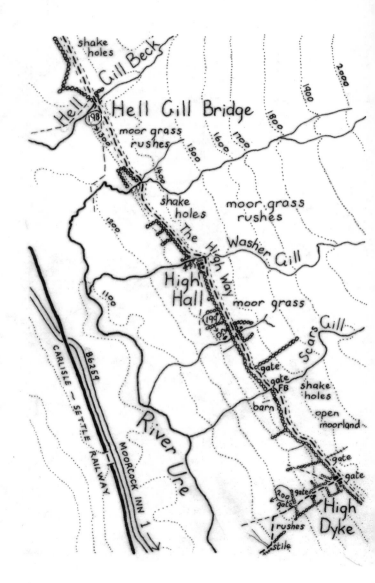

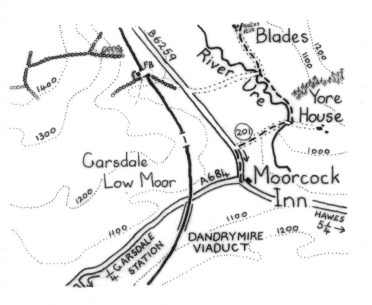

Look out for a wall stile close to the river by sycamore trees on the left and continue by the river until the approach road to Deepgill is reached. Cross Thrang Bridge and climb briefly to the B6259, turn right and almost immediately left onto a wide stony track (SP Public Way). This is an ancient track, used by the Lady Anne Clifford's Way encountered on Day 3, which climbs gently to 'Water Cut'. The track is followed without any problems to Hell Gill Bridge soon after which, at a fork, keep left. The High Way continues on to High Dyke where there is a crossing of paths. Turn right through the ruined farm buildings and descend through meadows bearing left to the farm of Blades. Here there is a choice of paths – take the one to the left, immediately before the first building to join the farm track. Follow the track to the first bend, where it crosses the Ure, but before the bridge keep left along the river bank. Upon reaching the farm road to Yore House turn right over the bridge, go up to the road and then left to the Moorcock Inn.

DAY SIXTEEN

Garsdale Head to Sedbergh

Distance	13¾ miles
Highest Point	1,450 feet
Height Ascended	1,949 feet
Going	Moderate
Map	O.S. Explorer OL19

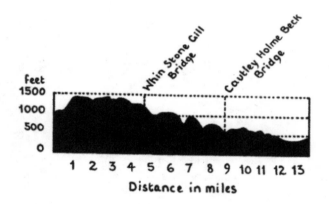

The Moorcock Inn was an important hostelry on the old thoroughfare from Hawes to Sedbergh and it is situated just beyond the head of Garsdale at the junction of this old road (now the A684) and the B6259 (Kirby Stephen road). It lies close to the major watershed from which rises the River Ure, which merges with the River Swale to become the River Ouse, before eventually reaching the North Sea at the Humber Estuary. Also from this watershed the Eden starts its journey towards the Solway Firth, as does a tributary of the River Lune, which flows into the Irish Sea and gives its name to the county of Lancashire.

The route crosses the Settle to Carlisle railway at the start and, after passing around Grisedale, heads for the desolate slopes of Baugh Fell.

Moorkcock Inn, Garsdale Head

This section of the route is not for the faint hearted as the underfoot conditions are challenging – sloping, wet, reedy terrain where the path is more on the map than on the ground. Rawthey Gill is seen as it descends from its source on Baugh Fell and then is followed to Uldale before becoming the River Rawthey. The path meets AW's 1938 route where it crosses the A683 (Kirkby Stephen to Sedbergh) – then the road was 'a narrow secondary road, but a good one' and he was to follow it almost into Sedbergh. This part of the Howgill Fells, which he may well have been seeing for the first time, he describes as 'majestic, having almost the grandeur of mountains'. He was particularly impressed by Cautley Crag 'a cliff almost a mile in length' and the waterfalls of Cautley Spout.

The Rawthey Valley is narrow and the path stays necessarily fairly close to the river passing the Cross Keys Inn at Cautley. This is a Temperance Inn owned by The National Trust, with a long-standing connection to the Quaker movement which continues to the present day. AW enjoyed the ham and eggs here, whilst he was writing *Walks on the Howgill Fells*, as is evidenced by his sketch in the book. The path continues beneath the fells

Cross Keys Inn, Cautley

until the valley widens on the approach to Sedbergh. Here it follows the riverside until the town is reached.

Route Description

From the Moorcock Inn return along the road towards Kirkby Stephen and opposite a footpath to Cotterdale leave the road by a gate on the left (BW Grisedale 1½m). Cross the Settle to Carlisle railway using the crossing gates or the footbridge. Pass to the right of the house, over the stile and climb the field, aiming to the left of a line of trees. The field is wet and reedy, with many nettles – not a place for shorts! Upon reaching the wall follow it to the left on steadily rising ground; ignore a gate on the right to arrive on the crest of the hill at a ladder stile and gate. Head slightly right across the meadow, to meet and follow a wall on the left to a broad, rutted track. This meets a metalled road but continue ahead on a stony track to pass a ruined barn on the left and a lime kiln on the right. Ahead is Flust, where the track passes through two gates and a ford between the trees. The

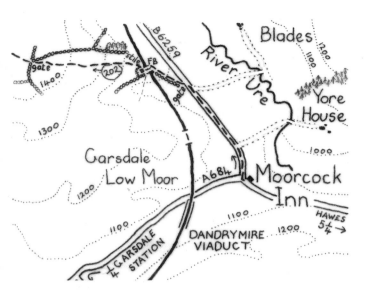

path, very wet in places, continues between a wall and a wire fence and rises to the right. Pass through a gate and over a stile and where the wall turns 90° left, walk up the bank to the right to locate a faint trod heading west. This track passes numerous shake holes on the right.

Where the path meets a rocky gill, head up the gill and keep straight on where it bends sharp right to locate another faint trod heading south-west. The 'path' continues across the wet, reedy hillside and in fog care should be taken to avoid the many shake holes. Stay above Rawthey Gill to meet a wall and locate a gate. In the absence of any visible track contour above the infant Rawthey aiming for conifers which shelter Dockholmes, a limestone gorge. The way continues across more wet, reedy ground staying above Rawthey Gill to reach, eventually, the peaceful surrounds of Whin Stone Gill Bridge. The route ahead is in a grooved track, and passing through a gate by a sheepfold aim for the trees ahead across firmer, grassy ground until a grooved track leads

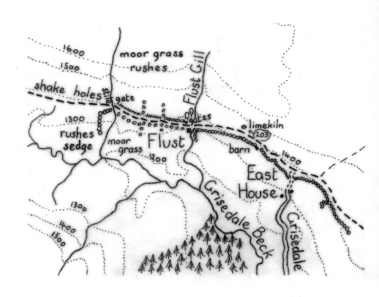

to Blea Gill Bridge in its woodland setting. On entering Uldale House farm take a gate on the right in the farmyard, before the farmhouse, leading onto the farm road.

Ahead are the Howgill Fells and on the right before a T-junction are shake holes, one of which is big enough to swallow a bus! At the junction a short green lane leads to a gate. Continue straight ahead, downhill, on a strip of land between walls with a zigzag path visible on the hillside ahead. A small footbridge gives access to the A683: cross the road and, slightly to the left, is a track (FP Murthwaite). Ascend the zigzag path seen earlier and arrive at a plank bridge and stile – do not cross, but, keeping to the right of the stream, continue up the hill to pass through a gate. Follow the fence on the left to meet a farm track heading left to Murthwaite. After a gate, a sign on the right (BW Narthwaite) points to a stony track to the right of a stone barn. The path finally becomes a stony descent into Murthwaite Park, through the trees, to ford Wandale Beck.

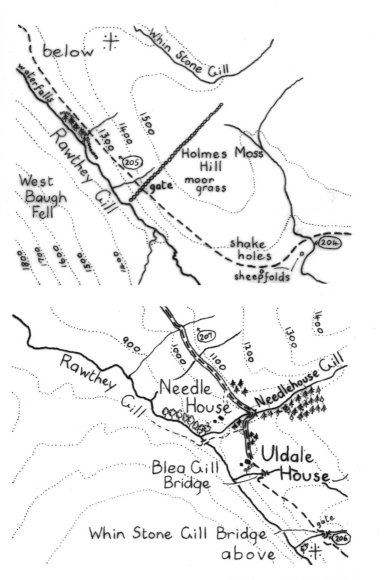

below ✝

Whin Stone Gill

waterfalls

Rawthey Gill

West Baugh Fell

1300
1400
1500
1800
1700
1600
1500
1400

205

gate

Holmes Moss Hill

moor grass

shake holes

sheepfolds

204

Rawthey Gill

900
1000
1100
1200
1300
1400

207

Needle House

Needlehouse Gill

Uldale House

Blea Gill Bridge

Whin Stone Gill Bridge above

gate

206

✝

Pass through the gate and on a well defined path rise to a line of trees and another gate. This leads to a track from Handley's Bridge; follow this to the right to Narthwaite. Here, go right through a gate into the yard and then left between barns, dropping on a well defined track to Backside Beck which must be forded. Once over the beck, head left and follow the path towards the banks of the Rawthey across which, via a bridge, lies the Cross Keys Inn. Join the tourist track to Cautley Spout coming up from the Cross Keys and follow this to a footbridge on the left over Cautley Holme Beck. The path continues, becoming terraced, across meadows to a bridge over Hollow Gill. Here, the path climbs slightly right to a gate, then through another gate to reach Rooker Gill. This delightful terraced path continues through gorse and bracken; ignore a stile on the left and continue through several gates.

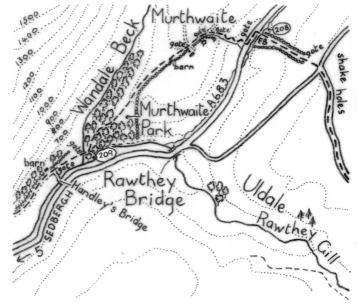

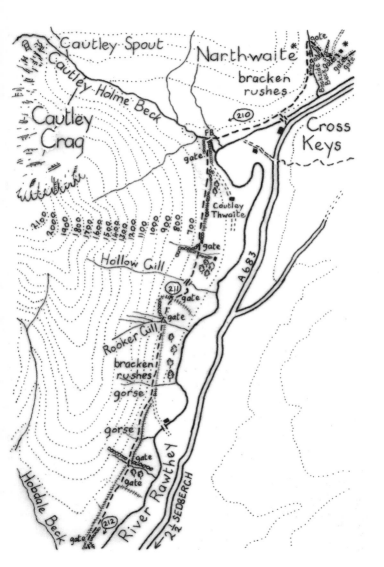

Cautley Spout

Cautley Holme Beck

Cautley Crag

Narthwaite*

bracken
rushes

210

FB

gate

Cautley
Thwaite

Cross
Keys

2100 2000 1900 1800 1700 1600 1500 1400 1300 1200 1100 1000 900 800 700

Hollow Gill

gate

211

gate

A 683

gate

Rooker Gill

bracken
rushes

gorse

gorse

gate

gate

Hobdale Beck

212

gate

River Rawthey

2½ SEDBERGH

On arriving at Fawcett Bank, keep to the left of the barn to join the access road down to the old stone bridge over Hobdale Beck. The track continues to Thursgill where it joins a metalled road which is followed to Buckbank.

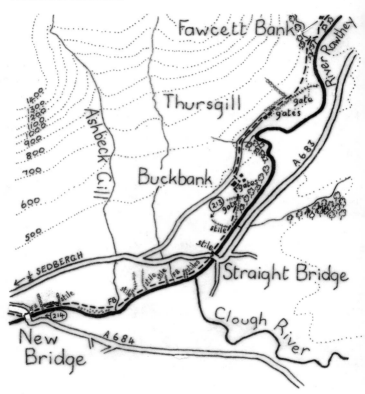

By the farm gate a sign (FP Straight Bridge ³⁄₈m) points through the yard to the right; go left between two block walls and gates leading to a meadow path. This leads down to the river and on over two stiles to the A683 at Straight Bridge. Cross the road and continue along the riverside path leading to New Bridge and the A684. At the parking area opposite, a footpath sign points down to the river and after a few yards turn right through a kissing gate and along a path skirting playing fields and tennis courts to meet a path. Turn left (FP Back Lane and Loftus Hill) passing a school on the right and go round the back of the Old Vicarage. With a playing field ahead, turn right to join the main road and then left to St Andrew's Church.

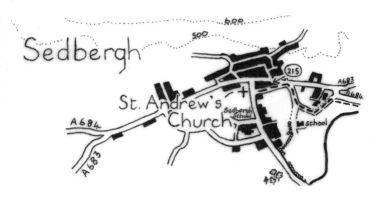

DAY SEVENTEEN

Sedbergh to Ingleton

Distance	17¾ miles
Highest Point	2,395 feet
Height Ascended	3,133 feet
Going	Strenuous with one long steep climb
Map	O.S. Explorer OL2 & OL19

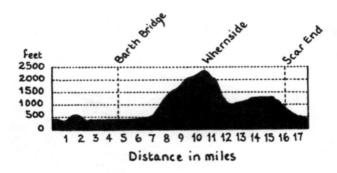

This stage is a delight from start to finish incorporating a lovely riverside walk, an ascent of one of the Three Peaks and ending with part of the very popular Ingleton Waterfalls Walk. In *Walks on the Howgill Fells* AW describes Sedbergh, which is a small attractive market town, as 'the capital of the region' but to many outside the area it is probably best known 'for the large Public School long established in its midst'. It is also well known to long distance footpath walkers as a staging post on the popular Dales Way which was encountered on the approach to Buckden early in the journey. The Dales Way is picked up on the outskirts of Sedbergh and followed along Dentdale where 'the river Dee threads the floor of the valley and plays hide and seek with you as you go along'. A short diversion from the river bank into Dent is highly recommended – the village, with its cobbled streets, is most attractive. In its centre is a huge block of granite which commemorates Adam Sedgwick (1785–1873), son of the local vicar, who was one of the founders of the science of geology. A memorial to him stands 'at the tiny crossroads in the tiny heart of the tiny town'. In his youth Adam Sedgwick would have been familiar with another local cottage industry – hand knitting. The poet Robert Southey wrote 'They er terrible knitters e' Dent', meaning they were excellent. The output of gloves, pullovers, caps and knee-length stockings was enormous, with a lot of it produced as men and women walked to their work in the fields and, it is said, while in church! In his last night's lodgings AW read, again, about the knitting industry of Dent. A more modern claim to fame for Dent is the local brewery whose reputation for traditional ales is spreading gradually across Northern England.

Whernside Summit

From Dent AW used the minor road that goes up Deepdale and down Kingsdale to Ingleton as this was his last day and he was making for Settle. Our route though is only to Ingleton and uses a combination of two of

AW's ascents of Whernside – 'a long high moor' – from *Walks in Limestone Country*. At Mill Bridge the path joins Walk 21 taking in part of the Craven Way (an ancient right of way that links Dentdale and Ribblehead) on its way to the summit. The descent uses part of the one in Walk 7 to Twistleton Hall before joining the popular Ingleton Waterfalls path, passing 'waterfalls, beautifully and bewitchingly set in wooded glades and rocky gorges'.

Beezley Falls

Route Description

From St Andrew's church take either of the two branches of the A684 road east through the town and where the two roads join, turn right down Vicarage Lane (FP Settlebeck or Millthrop). When the track swings left, go straight ahead through a kissing gate and follow a clear path, with a wall on the left, up the field to a kissing gate onto the drive of Winder House (Sedbergh School). Cross the drive to another kissing gate and descend the field with the school wall on the left. At the next field, go forward for only a few yards before turning right through a gated gap stile, and follow a clear path at first along the top of a steeply

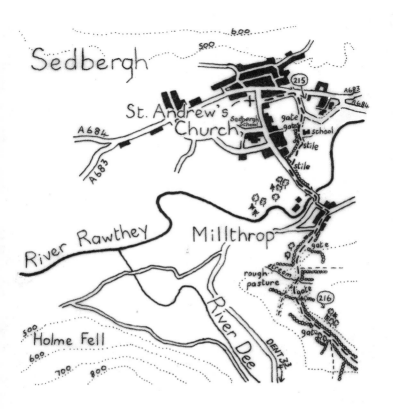

sloping pasture and then diagonally across the field to reach a road. Turn left to the bridge over the River Rawthey to rejoin the Dales Way for the next 6 miles. Follow the road round to the right then turn left up a lane (SP Millthrop). At the T-junction in the hamlet, turn right and at a right hand bend in the road, turn left on a walled stony track uphill (BW Frostrow Fell). Where the track forks, take the left hand branch to a gate in a wall to the right of a copse, from where the bridleway stays close to a wall to meet a walled lane and a gate. This delightful green lane has improving views of lower Dentdale on the right. At another gate enter Gap Wood and exit it at a gate and ladder stile. Cross the field on a clear path and then a short walled lane leading to Gap farm. Pass in front of the buildings (BW Brackensgill, FP Craggs Farm) and head down the farm track to the Dent road. Almost opposite but to the left a track (BW Brackensgill [Deep Ford]) drops down to the River Dee to a footbridge and onto the minor road at Brackensgill. Turn left along this lovely quiet road and soon after passing the footbridge at Ellers, take the path on the left to the riverbank.

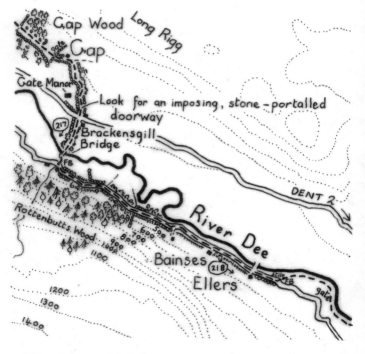

There is now a delightful riverside path with good views of Dent and at Church Bridge, Dent is a mere 300 yards away and well worth a visit.

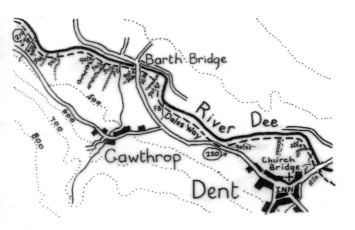

The path continues beyond Church Bridge, initially to the right of a small tributary, before turning left through a gate and returning to the riverside path. This is followed past the confluence of the river with Deepdale Beck and on to the road at Mill Bridge. *If bad weather prevents the ascent of Whernside, turn right and at the next road junction take the road left to Deepdale. This lonely moorland road which climbs to the head of the valley and then drops down Kingsdale leads directly into Ingleton — it is the route AW took from Dentdale.* Turn left over the bridge and leave the Dales Way by following the road uphill to a narrow tarmac lane on the right signed as a no through road. Pass the former Deepdale Methodist Chapel, now a private residence and take a stony track on the left (SP Craven Way and BW Ribblehead 3¾m) which passes through a gate and turns right up a wide walled lane. The track emerges from its walls and continues to a wall corner.

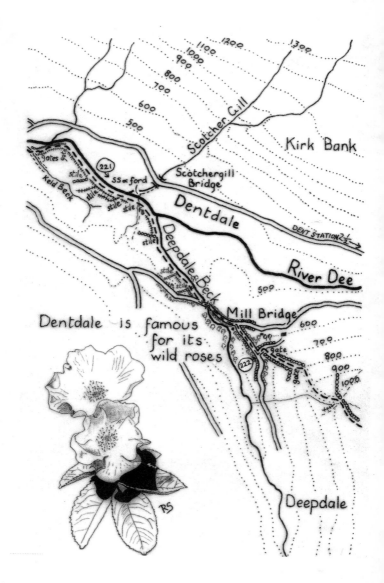

Dentdale is famous for its wild roses

RS

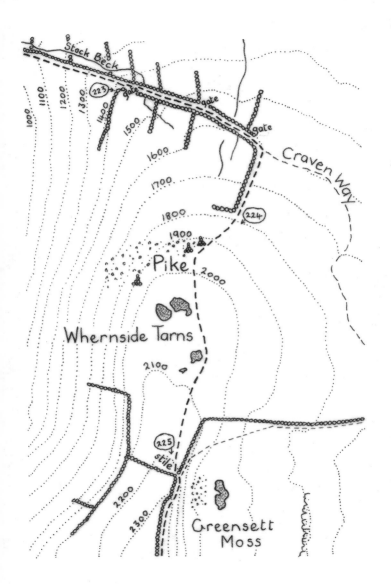

Stock Beck

1000 1100 1200 1300 1400 1500

223

gate

gate

gate

Craven Way

1600

1700

1800

224

1900

Pike

2000

Whernside Tarns

2100

225

stile

2200

2300

Greensett Moss

Follow the track uphill until the gradient eases and the path becomes walled again. At the second of two gates there is a lovely view of Dentdale and, in the far distance, the Lake District fells. Here the lane becomes a real green road – a pleasure to tread. Where the wall bends away leave the Craven Way, following the wall uphill to the right and where it turns right again take a narrow path straight ahead steeply uphill heading towards the two tall cairns on Pike. This path remains clear all the way to the summit ridge of Whernside and should not present problems, even in mist. On cresting a rise, the unexpected and attractive Whernside Tarns are reached with the summit ridge now in view. The path rises to a wall coming up from the left and, over an awkward wooden stile at a wall corner, arrives dramatically on Whernside's summit ridge. Turn right uphill on a very clear path – the Three Peaks route coming up from Ribblehead to the summit. From the summit can be seen the famous Ribblehead Viaduct, Ingleborough which will be encountered on the final stage of the Pennine Journey and, in the distance, Penyghent. The descent starts using the path along the wall through a kissing gate and, by virtue of being such a well trodden route, can be followed without any problems. The path drops quite steeply in places using pitched steps but after two gap stiles the gradient eases slightly, eventually reaching pasture which is crossed diagonally to a gate and ladder stile adjacent to a barn. Follow the rough lane round to the right (SP Hill Inn) and at a junction of tracks go straight ahead (BW Scar End 3½m). The track passes the ancient farmhouses of Bruntscar and Ellerbeck where, through a gate into the yard, turn left to pass to the left of the house. Turn left again, following the farm drive with a wall on the left, to reach a small plantation and cross Ellerbeck Gill.

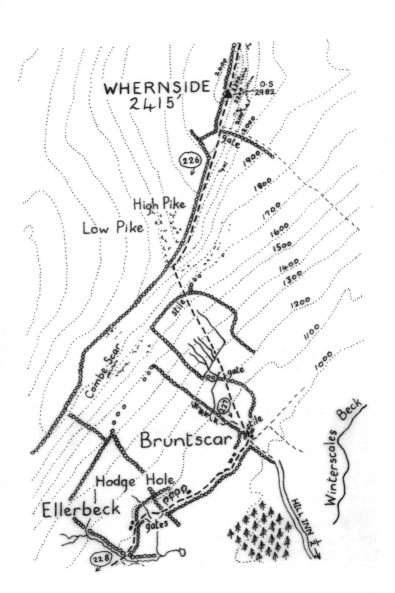

WHERNSIDE
2415'

O.S
2982

226

High Pike

Low Pike

gate

Combe Scar

stile

gate

227

stile

Bruntscar

Hodge Hole

Ellerbeck

gates

228

Winterscales Beck

HILL INN

Here, ignore the good track going left down the stream and follow the sign ahead (BW Scar End 3¼m). You have probably just walked the longest quarter-mile in England — it was only 3½ miles to Scar End back at Bruntscar! The track forks almost immediately; keep left, and the route soon narrows to a path. This ancient path, Kirkby Gate, will be followed for 3½ miles. It is often narrow and is almost always visible on the ground but walkers need to be attentive, particularly in mist. The path passes through a scar and after a striking, fluted pothole on the left makes purposefully for a definite nick in the skyline ahead.

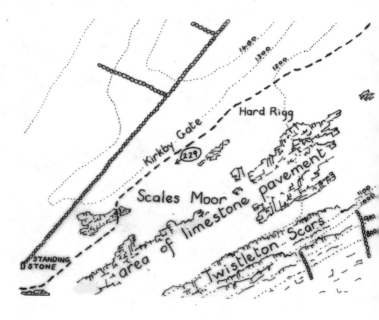

When this is reached the path becomes very clear and approaches a wall on the right before turning left to emerge from limestone onto an expanse of grass. Here, the route heads towards the right hand solitary tree. At a fork take the right hand branch and soon the path drops towards the wall but before reaching it, doubles back left (ignore a ladder stile ahead), to join a stony track. This is part of the very popular Ingleton Waterfalls Walk, which is followed into Ingleton. Turn left and descend to the two farms of Scar End and Twistleton Hall. Follow the signs for the Waterfalls Walk past the buildings and down to the road. Cross and take the drive opposite to the farm of Beezleys, then bear right and follow the signs for the Beezley Falls.

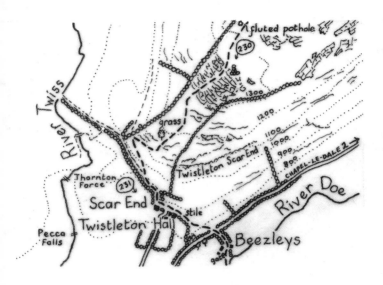

The highlights come quickly, with a succession of delightful waterfalls and only after the double cascade of Snow Falls does excitement subside as the path leads on through charming mature woodland. Emerge from the wood at a kissing gate and proceed straight ahead on a good track across Storrs Common (with a wonderful view back up the glen). The remains of buildings from a former quarry are passed on the left. The track becomes metalled leading into the village with the Youth Hostel on the right down towards the river.

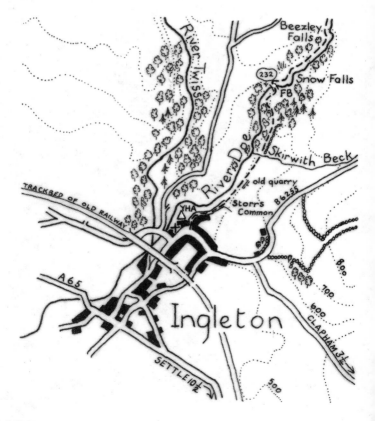

DAY EIGHTEEN

Ingleton to Settle

Distance	14¼ miles
Highest Point	2,369 feet
Height Ascended	3,081 feet
Going	Strenuous with one long steep climb
Map	O.S. Explorer OL2 & OL41

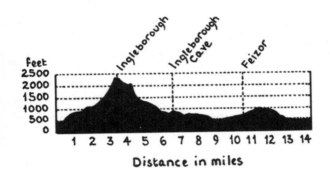

This last stage is truly a splendid finale to a varied walk. Also, fittingly, it has a particularly strong AW connection, being based largely on walks in this area described in *Walks in Limestone Country*.

Ingleton advertises itself as at 'the heart of the Three Peaks country'. It is certainly at the centre of this potholing and caving territory and so is extremely well situated for visitors, particularly walkers. But its seemingly tranquil setting and ambience belies its past. In addition to the quarrying that is still evident, it seems hard to accept that coal mining was a staple industry here with the only remnant being New Village – built for the miners and their families. Cotton mills, powered by a water mill, were in abundance. There is also a very famous literary connection. At nearby Masongill lived the mother of Sir Arthur Conan Doyle and, given the facts that there was a vicar of Ingleton named Sherlock and that the area below the splendid viaduct close to the centre of the village is called the Holmes, need one say more!

Crina Bottom and Ingleborough

Ingleton is left in the same manner as it was entered, by climbing one of the Three Peaks. Using routes that AW described and illustrated in *Walks in Limestone Country* the path makes its way over Ingleborough – 'probably the most ascended mountain in the country outside Lakeland'. The descent passes Gaping Gill, 'the best known of all British potholes', and a rival to Hull Pot which was encountered near the start of the journey. Gaping Gill is a massive natural underground chamber formed from the surrounding limestone, where Fell Beck plunges into a hole in the ground and drops 340 feet vertically into a chamber said to be large enough to contain York Minster. A little further is Ingleborough Cave which has been open to the public since floods in 1837 broke down calcite dams to reveal a wonderland of stalactites and stalagmites. Guided tours of the cave take place at regular intervals.

River Ribble, Settle

From Clapham the route roughly parallels the busy A65 but there is the quiet of Austwick, Feizor and Stackhouse to enjoy before meeting the Ribble at Langcliffe Mill. This area was much loved by the composer Edward Elgar who was introduced to it, at the start of his career, by a friend. A short walk near the river leads to the bridge on the outskirts of Settle with the station close at hand. The end of AW's Pennine Journey was marked by a double rainbow with 'a brilliant array of dazzling colours' through which he saw 'the roofs of Settle'. Such a sight may not greet you but, after resting tired limbs on one of the platform seats, you will experience that sense of quiet satisfaction which awaits all long distance footpath walkers at the end of their journey.

Route Description

From the Youth Hostel go towards the centre of the village and turn left along High Street to reach a T-junction and left again onto the B6255 Hawes road. *The road on the right to Clapham can be used as an alternative route should adverse weather conditions prevent an ascent of Ingleborough.* Soon afterwards take a stony track on the right (BW Ingleborough 2½m) which climbs across Storrs Common, initially following a stone wall on the right.

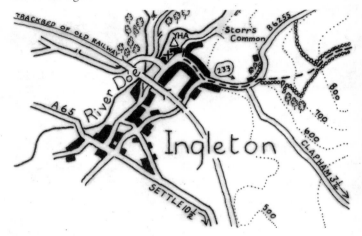

Then the well-defined track ascends the hillside and breasts a rise to become a walled track, Fell Lane. The track exits on to the open fellside through a gate and stile where a seat is well-placed on the left for those who would welcome a few minutes rest. At a fork approaching the farm at Crina Bottom go right (FP Ingleborough 1½m). This is a pleasant grassy path, passing the farm on the left with its stone boundary wall and accompanying, for a time, Hard Gill.

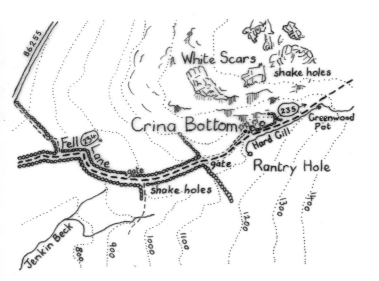

The path is always clear as it climbs the hillside. Near the top the path passes between cairns using well-pitched stone steps with a final steep, rocky assault through large boulders leading straight to the O.S. column. From the summit, a large plateau, there are good views of the other two of the Three Peaks. Once suitably rested, finding the route off the top is no easy matter in low cloud. A bearing of due east from the O.S. column helps to locate a cairn on the eastern edge of the plateau, visible in good conditions. Here turn sharp right heading due south to meet a low broken-down wall, believed to be Roman in origin. Cross this and soon find the path for the descent to Little Ingleborough — a pleasant grassy top with wide-ranging views. The clear path continues southeast, with part of the steep descent having pitched stone steps, and when more level ground is reached, at a fork, take the left branch to Gaping Gill which ought on no account to be missed, whatever the weather. The dangers of approaching the hole too closely are frighteningly obvious; don't!

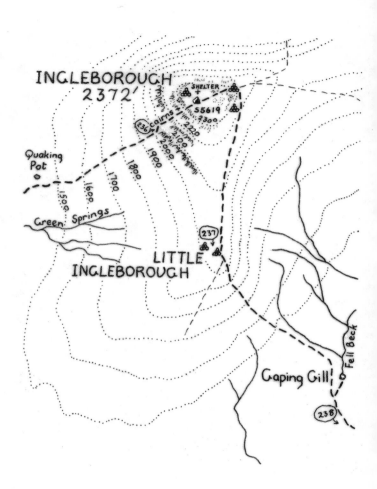

INGLEBOROUGH
2372'

SHELTER

SS619
2300

cairns

236

Quaking
Pot

Green Springs

LITTLE
INGLEBOROUGH

237

Gaping Gill

Fell Beck

238

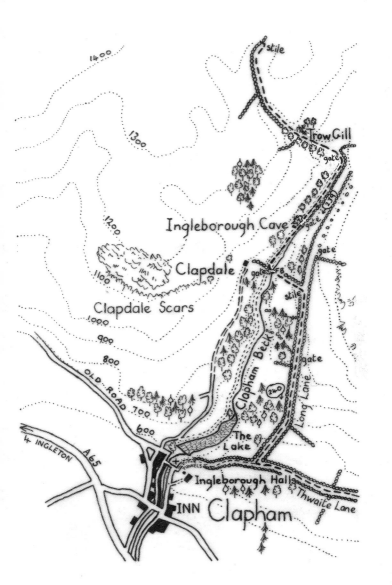

stile

TrowGill

gate

Ingleborough Cave

gate

Clapdale

gate

gate FB

Clapdale Scars

stile

gate

Clapham Beck

(two)

Long Lane

OLD ROAD

4 INGLETON

A65

TUNNELS

The Lake

Ingleborough Hall

Thwaite Lane

INN Clapham

1400
1300
1200
1100
1000
900
800
700
600

Rejoin the original path, go through a patch of limestone clints and take a grassy path to cross a double ladder stile. Turn right and follow the stone wall down a steep-sided grassy valley. At the end of the wall the path descends sharply over boulders into the narrow defile of Trow Gill. Then the route opens out again into a pleasant grassy valley, descending to a gate in a stone wall with an adjacent stile. The path now curves to the right with the wall on the left and leads unerringly to the entrance to Ingleborough Cave where refreshments are available. The pleasant level path continues alongside Clapham Beck until just before a gate entering Ingleborough Estate. Here take a thin path to the left over a footbridge to cross the beck. Keep close to the stone wall on the left and climb out of the valley to a stone step stile in the wall corner. Turn right onto the stony track, Long Lane, descending gently until woodland is reached where the track rises to a T-junction. Turn left on Thwaite Lane (BW Austwick 1½m).

This is a pleasantly undulating walled track with views opening up to the right, where the busy traffic on the A65 can be seen (and heard). Soon after passing a narrow belt of trees on the right, Long Tram Plantation, descend and take a waymarked ladder stile on the right into a field and, with a small beck on the left, cross the field to the corner and another ladder stile. Now, with a wall on the right, another ladder stile next to an old step stile and a quaint arched gate, leads to Townhead Lane. Turn right towards Austwick, go down to a T-junction and turn left. At the edge of the village the route again meets the Pennine Bridleway at a track on the right (BW Feizor 1¾m) immediately before a large stone barn. This leads down to a clapper bridge (Flascoe Bridge) and on to a junction of tracks. Here continue straight ahead, uphill, passing Wood House on the left. The now narrow walled track continues charmingly around twists and turns, passing ladder stiles to left and right, to a junction at the part-ruinous Meldings Barn.

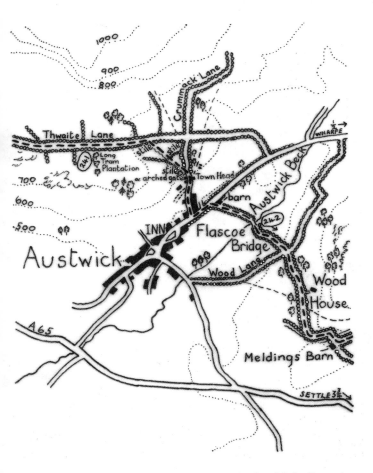

Take the left fork into Hale Lane, past Cat Hole Barn, into
Feizor. Go left (BW Little Stainforth 5¼m) and then, leaving the
Pennine Bridleway, right up a stony track (BW Scar Top 1⅓m; FP
Stackhouse 2m) through a gate and into open limestone uplands with
a wall on the left. Where the track heads away from the wall, keep

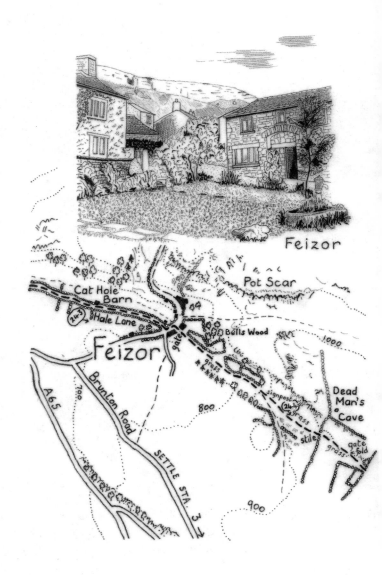

Feizor

Pot Scar

Cat Hole
Barn
Hale Lane
2¼3

Feizor

Bells Wood

gate

1000

Dead
Man's
Cave

signpost
2¼4

grass

stile

gate
& fold

grass

A65

Brunton Road

700

800

SETTLE STA. 3

900

straight ahead to meet another wall on the left. Where this wall turns away left at a lone tree, bear slightly right to an isolated signpost (FP Stackhouse 1½m; BW Buck Haw Brow 1m) at a fork. Go left, on an improving path, to a ladder stile and gate in a wall. Follow the green grassy sward straight ahead to a gate in a wall corner, from where the path continues much more clearly ahead.

After the next gate, almost immediately take a gate in the wall on the right and follow the obvious path by the wall. Once through another gate continue straight ahead on a grassy path, descending quite steeply to a gateway at a wall junction. Straight across the far side of the next field are two ladder stiles. Take the left hand one into a large pasture and, as there is no path on the ground, make directly for the village of Langcliffe visible on the far side of Ribblesdale. From the steep descent down a grassy bank can be seen an isolated signpost (SP Stackhouse Lane). Turn right and after shortly meeting a wall, keep straight ahead with the wall on the left and trees on the right. The path enters a meadow close to a road. Continue ahead, with the road on the left, to a stile leading onto the road with a gated stile (FP Giggleswick) opposite. Take this path across the field, through stiles, with Attermire Scar prominent across the river and Settle soon coming into view. More stiles bring the path level with the river and after skirting playing fields on the right, an enclosed footpath alongside Settle United AFC football pitch leads to the main road. Turn left over the Ribble and immediately right into Kirkgate which is followed, passing Settle Cricket Club on the left and Booths supermarket on the right. Turn right before the railway bridge into Bond Lane and when it meets Station Road turn left under the railway bridge to Settle station, and the end of this Pennine Journey.

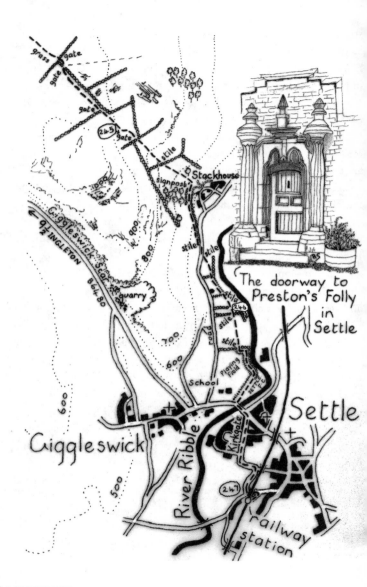

gross gate

gate

gate

243 gate

stile

Stackhouse

signpost

Giggleswick Scar

9½ INGLETON

864·80

quarry

stile

stile

The doorway to
Preston's Folly
in
Settle

stile

246

stile

road

stile

School

Playing
Field

Settle C.P.

Giggleswick

River Ribble

Kirkgate

Settle

247

railway
station

INDEX TO PLACE-NAMES

Numbers in *italics* relate to place-names on the maps.

POSTSCRIPT

Heather and I had mixed emotions when we arrived at Settle station at the end of the test walking – pleasure and relief but also a little sadness. Pleasure that we had reached another milestone on the journey of translating the vision we had nearly eighteen years ago into a published reality, relief that the 247 miles were, literally, behind us but also the sadness of knowing that, whilst we will no doubt reprise some sections of the walk, we will not repeat the walk again in its entirety.

The whole journey is undoubtedly a challenge and there are some sections that are very challenging – places where the path seems, and unquestionably is, more on the map (and here I include the OS maps) than on the ground. However, these parts are more than balanced by stretches where route finding is easy – by this I mean where the route coincides with established and already waymarked routes. I make no apologies for specifically mentioning the question of waymarking. I am confident that this journey will attract the attention and support of the long distance footpath walking fraternity. But to enhance its reputation will require the ongoing recommendations of LDP walkers and this can realistically only be achieved if the walk is an enjoyable experience. One measure of the enjoyment of walking any footpath, long or short, must surely be the absence of frustration – particularly the frustration that arises from losing your way and having to spend time and effort to get back on track. So it is my hope that, sooner rather than later, the various authorities through whose areas this journey passes will collectively agree a measure of basic waymarking. All royalties from the guide are to be set aside for route waymarks and path improvements.

It has been suggested that it should have been possible to mirror AW's 1938 route better using existing footpaths, and of course this is undoubtedly right. All I would say is that during the development of the 1998 route, there was never any thought of it being published. It was our personal and private tribute to AW and thus required, where it was appropriate, the use of any footpath with which AW was associated. Consequently there was never any intention of mirroring the earlier route.

In the 'Personal Notes in Conclusion' to his Coast to Coast Walk pictorial guide AW said 'The map of England is an oyster very rich in pearls. Plan your own marathon and do something never done before . . . '. If you have enjoyed this walk, then why not devise one of your own?

READER'S LOG OF THE JOURNEY

Date	Section	N.G.R.
	Settle station	SD 817 634
	Langcliffe	SD 823 651
	Stainforth	SD 821 674
	Dub Cote Scar Pasture	SD 826 710
	Horton in Ribblesdale	SD 811 720
	Hull Pot	SD 823 745
	Foxup	SD 873 768
	Yockenthwaite	SD 905 791
	Hubberholme	SD 926 783
	Buckden	SD 942 772
	Cray High Bridge	SD 944 797
	Stalling Busk	SD 916 859
	Bainbridge	SD 935 901
	Oxnop Beck Head	SD 941 941
	Gunnerside	SD 951 982
	Keld Bridge	NY 896 011
	Tan Hill Inn	NY 897 067
	East Mellwaters	NY 967 126
	Bowes	NY 992 136
	Deepdale Beck Bridge	NY 967 154
	Birk Hatt	NY 935 183
	Grassholme Reservoir	NY 929 216
	Middleton-in-Teesdale	NY 948 254

\multicolumn{2}{c}{Miles}		\multicolumn{2}{c}{Times}		Weather
S	C	A	D	
-	-			
1¼	1¼			
3¼	3¼			
6	6			
7¼	7¼			
2¼	9½			
6¼	13½			
9¾	17			
11¼	18½			
12¾	20			
1¾	21¾			
6½	26½			
10	30			
13½	33½			
17½	37½			
5¼	42¾			
9¼	46¾			
15½	53			
17½	55			
2¼	57¼			
6¼	61¼			
8¾	63¾			
12½	67½			

Date	Section	N.G.R.
	High Force	NY 880 283
	Saur Hill Bridge	NY 855 302
	Swinhope Head	NY 899 332
	Westgate	NY 908 381
	Rookhope Burn	NY 937 428
	Ramshaw	NY 949 472
	Blanchland	NY 966 503
	Slaley Forest entrance	NY 954 547
	Dukesfield Smelt Mill	NY 941 580
	Newbiggin	NY 944 608
	Hexham	NY 936 641
	Acomb	NY 933 665
	Chollerford Bridge	NY 920 705
	Mithraic Temple at Brocolitia	NY 859 711
	Housesteads	NY 789 687
	Caw Gap	NY 727 669
	Walltown Gap	NY 680 666
	Greenhead	NY 660 654
	Batey Shield	NY 654 608
	Burnstones	NY 676 546
	Kirkhaugh	NY 694 500
	Alston	NY 717 465
	Garrigill	NY 745 415
	Greg's Hut	NY 691 354
	Ranbeck Farm	NY 654 322
	Milburn	NY 656 294

| Miles | | Times | | Weather |
S	C	A	D	
5¼	72¾			
8¼	75¾			
12½	80			
15¾	83¼			
4¾	88			
8	91¼			
10¾	94			
3¼	97¼			
7	101			
9¼	103¼			
11¾	105¾			
2	107¾			
5¾	111½			
10¼	116			
15½	121¼			
4½	125¾			
7¾	129			
9¾	131			
4	135			
9½	140½			
13	144			
17	148			
4¼	152¼			
10½	158½			
14½	162½			
16¾	164¾			

Date	Section	N.G.R.
	Knock (C of E Mission Room)	NY 679 270
	Redbanks Bridge	NY 694 245
	Appleby Low Cross	NY 683 204
	Sandford Bridge	NY 727 158
	Musgrave Bridge	NY 766 131
	Belah Bridge	NY 794 121
	Kirkby Stephen	NY 775 085
	Lammerside Castle	NY 772 047
	Thrang Bridge	NY 782 005
	Hell Gill Bridge	SD 786 969
	Garsdale Head (Moorcock Inn)	SD 798 927
	Whin Stone Gill Bridge	SD 736 961
	Cautley Holme Beck Bridge	SD 693 968
	Sedbergh (St Andrew's Church)	SD 657 921
	Barth Bridge	SD 695 879
	Whernside	SD 738 814
	Scar End	SD 701 751
	Ingleton (Youth Hostel)	SD 696 733
	Ingleborough	SD 741 746
	Ingleborough Cave	SD 754 711
	Feizor	SD 789 676
	Settle station	SD 817 634

Miles		Times		Weather	
S	C	A	D		
2½	167¼				
4½	169¼				
8¼	173				
4½	177½				
8	181				
12¾	185¾				
16	189				
3	192				
6¼	195¼				
9	198				
12¼	201¼				
4¾	206				
9	210¼				
13¾	215				
4½	219½				
10¾	225¾				
16¼	231¼				
17¾	232¾				
3½	236¼				
6½	239¼				
10½	243¼				
14¼	247				

APPENDIX

Geof Avery
Peter Burgess
Graeme H. Chapman MBE
Richard Daly
David Figures
Derek & Hilary Grayson
Derek & Susan Hainsworth
Peter Hardy
John & Elizabeth Harvey
Geoff Houlton
Tony Huntington
Jill King
Martin Kirk
Andrew Leaney
Roy Male
David & Barbara Mawer
Don Morris
David Mould
Alan Nash
Caroline Nichol
Philip Powell
Ian Prater
Ron Scholes
Oliver Taylor
James Trevelyan
Keith Walker
Phillip Wickens
Diane & Chris Williams